Prison(er) Education

SECOND EDITION

Edited by Steve Taylor
Foreword by Barry Sheerman MP

Published by

Forum on Prisoner Education

Prison(er) Education
Second Edition

Published by	Forum on Prisoner Education Room 207 2 Abbot Street London E8 3DP
Telephone	0870 75 65 795
Fax	0870 75 65 796
Email	info@fpe.org.uk
Website	www.fpe.org.uk

ISBN   0954853857

A catalogue record for this book can be obtained from the British Library.

Printing and binding: Athenaeum Press Ltd., Gateshead. Tel 0191 491 0770. Typeset in Gill Sans. 'Forum on Prisoner Education' logo typeset in DearJoe.

Cover design by Antony Sanders at HMP Ranby, Nottinghamshire.

Contents

Acknowledgements

This book aims to add to the debate and awareness around prisoner education, a key role for the Forum on Prisoner Education and one highlighted by Barry Sheerman in his Foreword.

My biggest thanks are due to the nine contributors were faultless in providing their chapters on time and with a minimal need for editing – these are the people who have allowed the Forum, once again, to add to the debate. I owe thanks to Professor David Wilson, Chair of the Forum, for his advice on producing this second edition to the book he first edited with Dr Anne Reuss.

Barry Sheerman MP deserves special recognition and thanks; not only for his Foreword to this book, but also for his work and interest in penal affairs spanning many years, and for the scrutiny of prison education provided by his Committee. The Forum on Prisoner Education shares his frustration at the difficulty in raising the policy profile of the subject.

Keen to show the Forum's commitment to using the skills that exist in abundance in our prisons, we were very pleased to be able to use a cover design from a student at HMP Ranby in Nottinghamshire. We are very grateful to Antony Sanders, the designer, and to Sue Bance and Nigel Wharrier for facilitating the design process. The quality of the design demonstrates the talent so often wasted in our prisons.

Finally, a great deal of thanks are due to Rich King at the Forum on Prisoner Education for typing various parts of this manuscript and helping to manage the project, and also to Sharon Weir and the team at Athenaeum Press for guiding the book into print.

About the Contributors

Dr Phil Bayliss is Senior Lecturer in Continuing Professional Development in the Faculty of Education the University of Plymouth. His main interest is in the Continuous Professional Development of educators in prisons. He is a patron of UNLOCK – the National Association of Ex-Offenders.

Jill Clark is a Senior Research Associate based in the Centre for Learning and Teaching at the University of Newcastle upon Tyne. She has worked as an academic researcher for 13 years. Although now working in the field of educational research, Jill has a strong background in Social Sciences research. Her first degree is in Behavioural Sciences and she then completed her postgraduate degree in Criminology at the Institute of Criminology, University of Cambridge. Her professional interests focus very much on those educational issues and social factors which can be called 'out of school' and which are community-based, and her methodological focus is very much in the area of qualitative research approaches.

Claudia Gosse joined the Education Department of HM Prison Winchester as an ESOL volunteer, and later began teaching basic skills. Through classroom-based basic literacy delivery it became apparent to her that while prisoner-learners valued their basic skills education, most did not feel that it would improve their employment or further education opportunities on release, indicating a discrepancy between Government and stakeholders' views of prisoner education. She sought permission, as part of an MA(Ed) dissertation, to follow up for six months on a small group of prisoners returning to the Hampshire area on release.

Ian Hall is a Research Associate based in the Centre for Learning and Teaching at the University of Newcastle upon Tyne. He has worked as an academic researcher for 8 years. Although now working in the field of educational research, Ian has a strong background in Social Sciences research. His first degree is in Sociology and Social Research. He completed his post-graduate degree in Social Research at the University of Northumbria at Newcastle. His research orientation is social constructionist with an emphasis on power, control and resistance in institutional settings.

Daniel Hayward is a Policy & Research Officer at the Forum on Prisoner Education. He joined the Forum in 2005 as Development Officer, having studied for an MA in Criminology from the University of Wales, Bangor. He is an ex-offender and is beginning PhD studies on disclosure and criminal records and their impact on the reintegration of ex-offenders.

Emma Hughes is a lecturer in criminal justice at UCE Birmingham. She is currently undertaking PhD research into distance learning in prisons funded by the Prisoners' Education Trust. Emma is a founder member of the Forum on Prisoner Education, of which she remains a trustee.

Siân Ingleby studied languages at Royal Holloway, University of London and at the University of the West of England. Since 2002 she has been teaching Information Technology and providing open learning support at HMP Leyhill in Gloucestershire, in addition to which she works as an Advanced Practitioner for Strode College. She became a trustee and then Secretary of the Forum on Prisoner Education in 2005. Having gained a distinction in her PGCert (FE) in 2005, she is now working towards a Masters with Plymouth University and Strode College.

David Moseley contributes to a number of research projects in the Centre for Learning and Teaching at the University of Newcastle upon Tyne. As Reader in Applied Psychology he has initiated and managed several large- scale projects in educational and health contexts, working with voluntary bodies and public policy and research organisations. His publications include learning and assessment materials for use by children and adults, Open University course units and papers on: informatics, emotional intelligence, literacy, ICT, learning styles and constructs of teaching and learning. In 2002 he and his colleagues were funded by the Learning and Skills Research Centre to evaluate theories of thinking skills — work which led to an evaluation project focussing on oral communication and thinking skills interventions in prisons.

Barbara Schofield is a BBC radio producer and lecturer in broadcast journalism at City University London. She joined Radio for Development in 2003 as Prison Radio Project Manager at HMP Wandsworth. She is now contributing to the establishment of Prison Media at HMP Downview, where she will be working with female prisoners on the production of audio/visual materials for broadcast. She is also researching potential ways of delivering prisoner learning and encouraging creativity and the sharing of information in prisons through media in general and radio in particular. Her research is based on observations and experiences of the educational impact of creative broadcasting by prisoners at Wandsworth. Of particular interest are the educational and developmental benefits for prisoners of exploring voices and experiences in relatively unmediated broadcast forms like audio diaries, personal histories, poetry and plays.

Barry Sheerman graduated from the London School of Economics with a BSc in Economics and an MSc in Sociology. After working in industry, he went on to teach American Studies at the University of Wales, Swansea, from 1966 until 1979, when he became Member of Parliament for Huddersfield East. He has been MP for Huddersfield since 1983, and chair of the House of Commons Education & Skills Select Committee since 2001. His front bench roles have included both home affairs and education.

Noel 'Razor' Smith is a prisoner at HMP Grendon. His acclaimed autobiography was published by Viking in 2004. Of the book, Noel writes: The writing of *A Few Kind Words and a Loaded Gun* was a long and sometimes painful process that started the last time I was on the street, back in 1998. I had been released from Albany Prison, on the Isle of Wight, in August 1997, after serving a decade behind bars for armed robbery, possession of firearms, and prison escape. I was 37 years old, with no useful qualifications, no work record, and no prospects for the straight world, but I did have the perfect CV for getting back into crime. With my criminal record, dating back to 1975, and with my reputation as a "staunch" violent career criminal, I was considered an asset for any team of aspiring bank robbers. So, I once again took the easy route and went back to being an outlaw.

Steve Taylor is Director of the Forum on Prisoner Education. An ex-prisoner himself, Steve has written widely on criminal justice and penal affairs. He is clerk to the All Party Parliamentary Group on Learning & Skills in the Criminal Justice System, and a trustee of the Howard League for Penal Reform. He has studied Social Policy & Politics at the University of London, Goldsmiths College, and for an MA in Criminal Justice at UCE Birmingham. Steve is currently conducting research into the media and political response to the murder of James Bulger in England and Silje Rædergard in Norway. He was awarded The Longford Prize in 2005 for his 'outstanding contribution to social and penal reform'.

Foreword

Barry Sheerman MP

Current provision of prison education is unacceptable. Whilst the Government has provided a substantial increase in resources it is failing to fully meet its manifesto commitment to 'dramatically increase the quality and quantity of education provision'. (House of Commons, Education and Skills Committee report on Prison Education, March 2005)

Our Select Committee report on prison education was highly critical of existing provision but was barely picked up on by the media or anyone outside of the prison education sector. If we had been so critical of any other aspect of education provision it would have made the headlines. This is symptomatic of the neglect of prison education in the mainstream media, politics and public opinion. Indeed, our report stated that 'for many decades in this country.. [prison education] has been a very low priority for the Government as well as in the mind of the public'.

We took a wide range of evidence for our inquiry into prison education. In our evidence sessions in the House of Commons we questioned a large number of experts in the field. We also undertook several visits to prisons in the UK, Finland, Norway and British Columbia, and conducted an evidence session in a Young Offenders' Institution.

For anyone who looks into the issue of prison education it soon becomes apparent that there are serious failings in current provision. In the Government's recent Green Paper on the subject they described the challenge as 'stark'.

According to the Government's own figures, the link between poor educational experiences, unemployment and re-offending is striking. Those who have been failed by the education system fill up many of our prisons. Those who we continue to fail with inadequate education provision whilst they are in prison are more likely to go on to reoffend. Evidence we took from the Forum on Prisoner Education revealed that prisoners who do not take part in education are three times more likely to be reconvicted. The Social Exclusion Unit estimated the cost of recidivism to the tax-payer to be in excess of £11 billion in 2002.

It goes without saying that it is in the interests of society and our economy, as well as the prisoners themselves, to tackle this deep-rooted problem.

Bold political leadership is required to tackle the endemic problems identified by our Select Committee, the Government and others. We should therefore welcome proposals in the Government's Green Paper to make offenders, for the first time, a priority group in the plans of the LSC and other bodies.

There are serious challenges to these ambitious proposals. Our Select Committee recognised the problems caused by the 'churn' of prisoners, with a constant movement of prisoners between prisons and a large proportion of short-term prisoners. This 'churn' combined with overcrowding in many prisons poses particular challenges to the practical delivery of education in prisons.

Prison education does not exist in isolation and must be considered in the wider context of probation and rehabilitation. The Government's proposals are largely dependent on the success of the National Offender Management Service which is still undergoing significant restructuring - about which there is currently much concern in the sector.

Additional resources will be needed to back up any proposals. With other areas of public services struggling to meet tighter budgets, there will need to be a clear consensus amongst policy-makers and the public opinion that we should prioritise prison education.

There has been a consensus in British Columbia about the importance of investment in rehabilitation since the 1930s which they were able to build on to introduce an effective system of prison education. A similar consensus exists in the Scandinavian countries to great effect. The subdued reception our report received shows that we have a long way to go to achieve such a consensus in this country and to convince the media and public opinion that prison education should be a high priority.

The Forum on Prisoner Education provided invaluable information for our Select Committee inquiry. This book and the ongoing work of the Forum are essential to informing debates and increasing the priority of policy on prison education.

Barry Sheerman MP
Chair of the Education & Skills Select Committee
House of Commons

March 2006

Introduction

Steve Taylor

I recently spent a few days at a city centre prison holding upwards of five hundred remand and sentenced adult male prisoners. It suffers the common pressures of a 'local' such as chronic overcrowding and a high turnover of prisoners.

On my first visit, the Head of Learning & Skills (HOLS) was keen to show me the prison's new 'Learning Centre'. It was a newly built, multi-million pound facility in no way different from a modern college save for the barred windows and gates. The HOLS was very proud – quite rightly – of the new building, not least because of her direct involvement in its design and success at persuading the prison's management of the potential return on the investment involved.

The Learning Centre had yet to open – prisoners would begin using the facility two weeks later – and a small opening ceremony had been planned. I asked if the local press were invited. They weren't. Not because the HOLS hadn't thought to invite them, but because she was concerned that reporting might lead to complaints at millions of pounds being spent on a new building, computers and interactive whiteboards for prisoners when, as the media might report, schools are 'crumbling'.

This is indicative of a wider problem. Various studies (a number of which were commissioned by the *Rethinking Crime & Punishment* initiative of the Esmée Fairbairn Foundation) have demonstrated how the 'general public' are in general agreement that the purpose of prison is to rehabilitate and ensure that prisoners, when released, do not reoffend. But such views are not represented in the media, for whom the staple diet of stories on prisons tends to focus on easy scaremongering. Witness, for example, the screaming front page of *The Mirror* on 8th March 2006 which told of how prisoners at HMP Belmarsh are being provided with laptops to help them prepare their legal paperwork. It was, according to that newspaper at least, 'disgraceful' and a 'dangerous waste of money'.

Readers of this book are unlikely to need converting to the more sensible view of how prisoners ought to be treated. But organisations such as the Forum on Prisoner Education face such opposition on a daily basis. Why spend money on criminals when children's education is in dire need of investment? The answer, that by investing in prisoner education we reduce the number of crimes and therefore victims is, it sometimes seems, too complex.

The Forum on Prisoner Education is a real 'Forum'. It exists to campaign and press for change like any pressure group, but also seeks to bring into the debate everyone concerned with 'offender learning and skills'. That includes prisoners, tutors, prison management, probation, the voluntary sector, colleges, training providers, civil servants, and parliamentarians, among others. We exist to broaden and raise awareness of the issue and to promote balanced and sensible debate: this book is an integral part of that work.

David Wilson (a former prison governor and now professor of criminology) and Anne Reuss (lecturer in criminology) edited the first edition of *Prison(er) Education* in 2000. It became something of a manifesto for the Forum on Prisoner Education, and most of its contributors signed up as founding members. Six years later, with three hundred members and a rapidly increasing staff, the Forum has proved the need for an organisation to concentrate solely on this vital aspect of penal policy. The Forum has become pivotal in increasing the awareness of prisoner education and ensuring that both sides of the argument are heard. Indeed, my work on this as Director of the Forum was one of the factors singled out for particular recognition by the judges of the Longford Prize.

I was delighted when Barry Sheerman MP agreed to provide the Foreword to this book. The Commons' Education & Skills Committee began its inquiry into prison education when I was just five months into this job, and on a steep learning curve that continues to this day. That Committee's work quickly became manna from heaven when their detailed investigation revealed the true state of prison education with far more gravitas and influence than the Forum could ever hope to achieve. Keen not to loose the parliamentary interest in prison education generated by the Select Committee's work, the Forum worked with a number of parliamentarians to create the All Party Parliamentary Group for Learning & Skills in the Criminal Justice System. The interest in that Group would have been minimal without the Committee's work.

This book aims to add to that debate, providing a précis of recent research and policy developments by a range of individuals in the sector. It is hoped that the Forum on Prisoner Education will publish a new edition on a regular basis; perhaps every two years.

The Chair of the Forum, David Wilson, has recently asked how the public would react to schools that failed to educate three-quarters of its pupils, or to a hospital that killed three-quarters of its patients. Both would be closed, and a bottom-up reform would follow, looking at the reasons for such failings. And yet, in our prisons which fail to stem the offending behaviour of between fifty and eighty per-cent of their clients, the public appear to sit back, unconcerned.

This book should add to that debate and show how, in the right circumstances, prisoner education can provide one of – if not *the* – most effective means of reducing reoffending and ought therefore to be given the highest priority by government, whose responsibility it is to inform the media and ensure that it is not only the reader of this book that needs no convincing of the value of prisoner education, but members of the public.

Steve Taylor
Director, Forum on Prisoner Education

April 2006

Inside Education

Siân Ingleby

Introduction

As part of my Postgraduate Certificate in Further Education at the University of the West of England, I was required to undertake a small scale research project. Having been employed for several years in prison education, I was eager to explore issues relevant to my students and their context as prisoner students. Working in prison education, I find myself asking internal questions on a daily basis – what have prisoners done to end up here, did they have family support whilst at school age, did they attend school on a regular basis, and does the age and/or sentence duration of the prisoner affect their motivation? A major difficulty therefore was choosing the direction of my enquiry and which questions to ask. Reading around the subject revealed many interesting possible avenues and seemed to exacerbate my dilemma.

My research was conducted in a Category D open prison. I was keen to effect an inquiry with the potential of benefiting our education department as a whole, evaluating the quality of our provision and highlighting areas we could develop and improve. I wanted to discover if we were actually delivering the courses the prisoner students desired, in the way they desired. Were there "gaps" in our provision? By means of a small scale inquiry, I accepted that I could not hope to obtain all the answers to my varied questions and decided to restrict the enquiry to three key areas – qualifications, motivation, and evaluation. This three pronged approach would enable me to assess views regarding the provision (evaluation) whilst permitting me to investigate the starting-points of prisoner students (qualifications) and satisfy my curiosity as to their personal motivation. It was also my intention to compare my findings with those of relevant agencies and academics.

My main source of literature research was *Prison(er) Education* – *Stories of Change and Transformation* (Wilson and Reuss, 2000) which grouped essays from various experts in the field, including academic researchers, related charities, and an ex-prisoner. It was recent and relevant to my study, containing invaluable comparisons. I also accessed briefing documents, press releases and links to Government and agency data through the Forum on Prisoner Education.

Methodology

In order to gather information for this project, I compiled a questionnaire and distributed it to fifty prisoner students attending education in the prison. I limited the numbers to have a realistic chance of collating the information effectively, whilst hopefully creating a large enough sample to allow useful conclusions to be drawn and trends to develop. This was followed up by semi-structured interviews with ten per-cent of the sample.

The first page of the questionnaire explained in an open and accessible manner my purpose and status as a researcher. In this environment, prisoner students are frequently loath to express frank opinions which they fear may prejudice their sentence planning. They rapidly learn to 'play the system', saying what they believe is expected of them rather than necessarily what they actually feel. In his "Evaluator's Tale", Ray Pawson speaks of the need of many prisoners to provide 'socially desirable answers rather than admitting the researcher into their true thinking' (Wilson and Reuss, 2000).

With this in mind, I stressed the need for congruency. I wanted to reassure recipients of it being an independent survey, for my own educational benefit, as well as possibly their own. It was an opportunity for them to influence future educational provision by stating their needs and ambitions. I indicated they did not have to answer any questions they were uncomfortable with and that I was willing to help if required: many prisoner students have low literacy skills and I needed to offer support to avoid alienating this element of the population.

The cover page had the additional benefit of providing confidentiality over the answers and names behind. The cover page also stipulated that the blank reverse pages of the questionnaire allowed the respondent to expand upon their responses in more detail if they so wished. Ten questions were spaced over two pages. I felt this was sufficient to cover relevant questions without being off-putting. A previous prison survey was criticised by prisoners for being too lengthy and some commented that "you had to have a degree to read it". I was keen to avoid both accusations.

The questionnaire merged my three-pronged approach. Firstly enquiries regarding qualifications; those gained prior to prison, whilst in prison, and a personal evaluation of courses either completed or in progress in this prison. The opportunity followed for those prisoner students undertaking independent and external courses to assess their importance and ease of access. Whilst many students in this context have low level basic skills, others are working towards high level qualifications. I wanted to cover all shades of the prison population spectrum. One particular question was key in regard to evaluation, enquiring whether there were courses they felt the education department should be offering. The remaining questions focused upon motivation, preferred learning styles and their evaluation of the quality of educational provision in the department.

It was my intention to produce quantifiable results whilst providing the opportunity for more qualitative responses. I therefore combined rateable and tick-box questions with open-ended questions allowing for fuller explanation. I was able to graph the results of the quantifiable questions and explore the reasoning behind the open questions, developing this further through subsequent interviews. I hoped then to compare my data and findings with relevant research studies and statistics concerning prison education.

Some questions inevitably proved problematic. Being conscious of the need for this enquiry to be accessible to all literacy levels, I was careful to word questions in a simple fashion yet avoiding a patronising approach which may have equally disengaged more educated students. The rateable questions were the most difficult to word in a succinct but comprehensible manner, ensuring that true results were obtained rather than misleading responses due to misunderstanding. Once my provisional questionnaire was drawn-up, I piloted it with five prisoner students of different educational levels. This was to gauge whether the questions were relevant and, importantly, easy to understand.

I did not overtly select the respondents of the enquiry. However, for the sake of convenience, I did distribute the majority of questionnaires personally to the different students in my daily classes. These were mainly prisoner students undertaking computer classes and those studying a variety of courses through open learning, where students study a wide range of subjects through distance learning at different levels, some up to PhD. The personal approach was to encourage a high return rate. As Anne Reuss discovered during her time as a prison education researcher 'a mutual working relationship needs to be built-up in order to proceed, using tools of diplomacy and tact' (Wilson and Reuss, 2000). Prisoners will often avoid non-obligatory tasks and my awareness of all this informed my approach.

My personalised approach proved justified. Questionnaires unreturned or incomplete were mainly those distributed through colleagues. The overall return was 70%. Despite my endeavours, some rateable questions were misread and I deemed those answers unquantifiable. However, the majority of questionnaires were thoroughly and, it would seem, accurately completed.

Eleven per-cent of respondents did not provide their names. A low percentage in terms of the prison environment which is by nature one marked by mistrust. This did not constitute a problem but exempted them from the interview stage. Twenty-three per-cent of respondents had either been released or transferred to another prison by the interview stage.

Although some prisoners are with us for several years, there is a large short-term element to the population. Some of the respondents were unable to provide a realistic assessment of our education provision due to lack of experience.

Similarly I only had access to prisoners who themselves accessed education. The population of the prison in the survey is several hundred men, however only a proportion of prisoners will choose to utilise the educational facilities. It must also be considered that the results of my enquiry were skewed by my sample being derived from prisoner students mainly attending computing and open learning courses. Such respondents are likely to have higher literacy and numeracy levels than statistics published by the Social Exclusion Unit in 2002 suggest.

Interviews were conducted with five respondents in a semi-structured format. I selected respondents to develop a deeper understanding of the opinions expressed within their questionnaires and they were all prisoners who showed an interest and appreciation of the study's purpose. These respondents also met my criteria of illustrating the wide spectrum of educational diversity in the prison.

The interviews were not audio recorded to avoid feeling threatening within the prison context. I was careful to assure interviewees of confidentiality. They are referred to as Respondent A, B, C, D and E. As issues discussed were of a purely educational nature, I was not compromising myself with respect to security and my professional obligations in this setting.

Discussion of Results

Qualifications

In order to form an overview of the 'starting-points' of the prisoner students, initial questions focused on two criteria; qualifications achieved prior to imprisonment and qualifications achieved at previous prisons. According to the return, 24 (69%) of the respondents had achieved GSCE/"O" Level grades or above prior to prison. 29% had "A" Levels, 31% degree and/or postgraduate qualifications. 34% had professional qualifications of some description. Only 14% of respondents had achieved no qualifications before imprisonment. *Fig. 1* illustrates these findings.

These results differ greatly from the findings of the Social Exclusion Unit (2002), where half of all prisoners were at or below the level expected of an eleven year-old in reading, two thirds in numeracy, and four fifths in writing. Over half of all male adult prisoners had no qualifications at all.

My results reflect a small cross-section of the prison population as opposed to the large scale enquiry above. As stated earlier, I only had access to prisoners attending education and furthermore my main sample was drawn from prisoners who would require a reasonable level of learning in order to undertake computing and/or open learning sessions. Whilst interesting in a localised context, it is possible that these findings do not extrapolate to the wider prison population.

Figure 1

Qualifications Gained Prior to Imprisonment

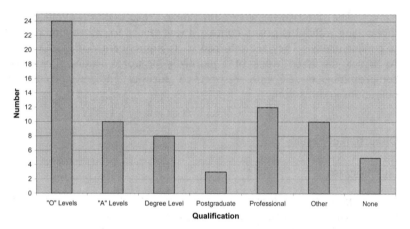

Qualifications gained at previous prisons, shown in *Fig. 2*, highlight the most popular courses, that of basic skills and computers. Fifty-four per-cent of respondents had achieved qualifications at previous prisons, of which 38% were in Level 1 or 2 basic skills.

It must be taken into consideration that some respondents, due to the nature of their crime, may not have attended another more secure prison for long enough to become engaged in education classes. Similarly the high computer score may be a reflection that after having attended computer classes in one prison, an prisoner would wish to continue his development in open conditions. My sampling 'by convenience' may have influenced this result.

Respondent E was a rewarding case study and was selected for interview mainly for the 'value-added' nature of his case. Entering prison with no qualifications, he seized on opportunities available to gain more than twenty certificates. Amongst others, he obtained Level 2 in numeracy and literacy, Level 3 computing and 'Firmstart' (business planning) qualifications. For someone with no previous educational achievement, his progress was remarkable. Before being released he had undertaken several 'AS' and 'A' Level History units and an onerous external NEBOSH (National Examination Board in Occupational Safety and Health) course. His whole working week was devoted to study, which he completed diligently, quietly, with single-minded focus.

Figure 2

Qualifications Gained at Previous Prisons

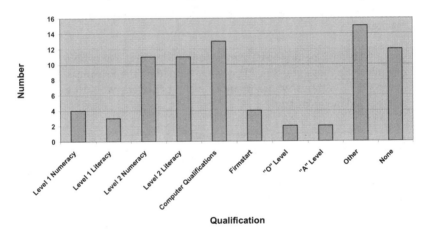

Respondent A perhaps illustrated the opposite end of the educational scale. He entered prison with postgraduate qualifications and felt there were no courses of value to him. However he used his time constructively in improving his foreign language skills independently in open learning sessions. His goal was to be accepted at a prestigious school for music and drama on release. This he achieved.

Detail within the questionnaires revealed a wealth of variety in courses undertaken by prisoners at previous prisons. Subjects included: 'A' Level English, art, cookery, bible study, assertiveness, psychology, welding, access to journalism, business administration, woodwork, craft design technology, biology and law.

Qualitative questions regarding independent and external courses (when prisoners are released daily under strict conditions) offered interesting insights. Over 57% of respondents were undertaking such courses, perhaps unsurprising as many of my sample were attending open learning sessions. Of these returns, twelve were broadly speaking academic, and ten vocational courses. Some respondents were undertaking courses in both categories. 'Academic' courses included foreign languages, mathematics, psychology, sociology, history, law, English literature, zoology, computer science and design. 'Vocational' courses varied from LGV (light goods vehicle) certificates, plumbing, electrical installation and NEBOSH, to counselling, teaching certificates, book keeping, and computer maintenance.

Several respondents expressed gratitude at being able to attend or undertake these courses. Many were funded by the Prisoners' Education Trust (PET) without whose support many prisoners would be unable to attempt independent study.

Other respondents were unable to access courses due to a combination of funding and/or security issues. The prison has a limited budget and strict criteria for day release. Respondent C was vociferous on this issue. He felt he had shown sincere commitment to educating himself through undertaking 'A' Level Psychology, yet he was unable to access several external courses. He had been refused ECDL (European Computer Driving Licence, a Level 2 computing qualification), NEBOSH and forklift courses. On investigation, the reasons for refusal were not personal as he understood it, rather financial, but nonetheless frustrating for him. One foreign national expressed disappointment at being unable to access external courses due to a perceived risk of him absconding; another Open University student had been thwarted in his progress by the ICT facilities in the department, which at the time were outdated.

Motivation

What motivates prisoners to attend education? I asked respondents to select their top three motivating factors and allocate them a score. *Fig. 3* illustrates the results.

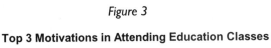

Figure 3

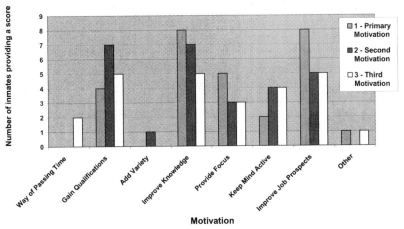

'Chance to improve knowledge' scored the highest with eight prisoner students naming it as their primary motivation, twenty students providing a score. 'Improve job prospects' also scored eight as primary motivation with an overall score of eighteen. 'Gain qualifications' figured highly with four students naming it as their primary motivation and sixteen allocating it a score.

Lesser motivations were: 'Gives me a focus', score of eleven, and 'Keeps mind active', score of ten. The options of 'Way of passing the time' and 'Adds variety' both generated low scores. 'Other' responses included "I enjoy learning", "nice to see smiling faces", "helping others" and "to help my daughters with their schoolwork". The first comment came from Respondent D who had held senior director positions in industry. He explained that he had no need to acquire additional qualifications but wanted to keep himself from vegetating. The third comment came from a prisoner who was undertaking basic skills and ESOL (English for Speakers of Other Languages) teaching qualifications. Unfortunately this was a problematic question. Thirty-one per-cent of the respondents did not complete it correctly and I was unable to compute their data.

Motivation is the focus of Petra MacGuiness' essay, *Dealing with Time: Factors that Influence Prisoners to Participate in Prison Education Programmes* (Wilson and Reuss, 2000). She discusses learning and academic achievement being 'valuable tools in overcoming the psychological instability of imprisonment' and raising the prisoner's self-esteem. Her conclusions led her to identify the following main motivation categories:

1. Starting education to catch up (54% of respondents);
2. Starting education to keep occupied;
3. Starting education to improve employment prospects; and
4. Starting education to survive prison and to manage the given time.

Age and sentence duration influenced the responses. Prisoners serving life-sentences appeared less concerned with gaining academic qualifications and improving job prospects, it being suggested that this was irrelevant to their situation. No replies were received from prisoners between 20-24 years of age whilst the 25-34 age group was the most responsive. This reiterates Ray Pawson's conclusions (Wilson and Reuss, 2000); he favours a 'maturity' hypothesis where in this latter age group prisoners have grown tired of the 'revolving door of reincarceration' and are prepared to work towards legitimate goals. Positive results were obtained from the pre-21 age group with it being suggested that they were seeking to avoid becoming 'ensconced in criminal culture'. The 22-30 age group was least likely to benefit from education; seemingly they had become 'ensconced' and were yet to gain the 'maturity' to wish to take positive action. Cultural as well as age factors were also viewed as significant by Pawson. This was not an area which I was able to explore within this study.

Evaluation

From the viewpoint of the education department, this was the most significant section as I hoped to highlight areas which could be improved, locating possible omissions in the current provision. One question listed the courses available and requested a score where applicable to that prisoner student. *Fig. 4* shows the results. Other questions relevant to this section required an evaluation of different elements of the provision and explored preferred learning styles. One qualitative question asked respondents to list any courses they would like to see provided and to explain their reasoning.

Figure 4

Evaluation of Courses Attended

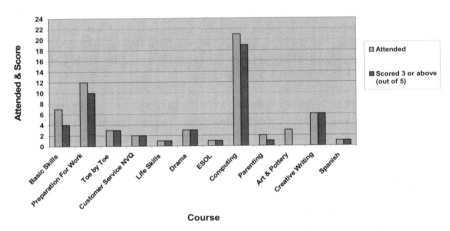

The results of *Fig. 4* are encouraging as most courses score three or above. Of the twelve courses available at that point in time, respondents for seven of the courses unanimously allocated high scores. Only one course, Art & Pottery, did not achieve an above three score. Inevitably, considering my sample, 60% of respondents had attended computer classes. Of these, 91% gave a score of three or above. Another popular course was Preparation for Work; 34% of the respondents had attended this course and 83% gave a positive score.

Whilst the computer course provision scored highly, it was an area perceived to be ripe for further development. Twenty-three per-cent of respondents expressed the wish to undertake courses in web page design, internet and email, specialist software, networking, computer maintenance or ECDL (European Computer Driving Licence). ECDL is requested frequently. Many prisoners have partially completed the qualification at previous prisons and arrive in open conditions hoping to achieve the full certificate by gaining an internet/email based module. Despite being an open prison, no prisoners have internet or intranet access and therefore would be unable to undertake this module. Furthermore, at the time of the survey, we were unable to offer this course due to budgetary restrictions.

When the questionnaires were circulated, the computers in the department were old, slow and outdated. We were still running the Microsoft Windows '95 operating system and could not offer many specialised courses due to its antiquity. Several respondents remarked on the inadequacy of these resources. Fortunately the computer suite has since been updated which will enable us to deliver a wider variety of design and graphics courses, if funds are available.

Other courses which were suggested by prisoners were: Firmstart, woodcraft, foreign languages, music courses, engineering, electrics and car mechanics. Respondent D suggested woodcraft to "provide a stimulating/creative course to work alongside my practical knowledge and skills. I also think this would be of benefit to anyone as it provides useful skills."

One student requested a "business start-up course as it will provide the skills needed to get self-employed once released". Subsequent to the survey, the Firmstart course was re-introduced and interest was high. Suitably qualified prisoners began teaching Spanish and French. It was also commented that evening classes would be beneficial, especially for those prisoners who are 'working out' of the prison during the day. This has since been rectified with drama, art and French currently being provided on one evening per week.

One student requested a course in Primary Education. Due to the nature of some prisoners' offences, this would not be seen as appropriate. It is also unlikely that there would be sufficient interest in such a qualification to warrant its provision.

As examined earlier in the 'Qualifications' section, many prisoners were undertaking a variety of vocational and non-vocational qualifications, either by private study in education, or externally by controlled day release. The 'Powerscheme' is a programme, initially run by education but now by the prison, which aims to help prisoners attend external courses. Funding and security limitations are often an issue but several prisoners were appreciative of the support they had received.

Feedback on the quality of provision was also heartening. As illustrated in *Fig. 5*, I requested scores for different elements within our provision. Each element had a possible highest score of 175. 'Quality of Support' scored highest (145) and was followed by 'Quality of Teaching' (132). Resources, variety and availability of courses achieved the lowest scores.

Figure 5

Evaluation of Education Provision

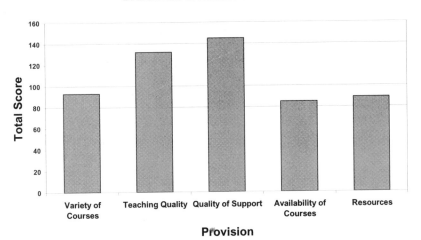

Striking an effective balance within prison education is an unenviable task. The Offenders' Learning and Skills Unit (OLSU) at the Department for Education & Skills (DFES) sets out a core curriculum which includes basic skills, key skills, ESOL, ICT, generic preparation for work, social and life skills. Tight budgetary constraints and key performance target (KPT) pressures limit provision and flexibility. In our department we would like to offer some valuable courses, such as ECDL, but cannot afford to do so. One respondent was particularly lucid on this issue, writing:

> The education department and staff do not get the economic, logistic and general support they need and deserve from the prison authorities if they are to fulfill the expressed (but not operated) doctrine of rehabilitating the offender.

There are often waiting lists for courses. The computer class, for example, has a two to three month wait before longer-term prisoners can gain access. I prioritise short-term prisoners to help them achieve a qualification before release. According to Professor David Wilson, of the total prison population of 75,000, education departments are only able to offer places to between one-quarter and one-third of that number (Wilson, 2004).

The questionnaires contained many positive comments about the education department. One prisoner student remarked: "The staff are very helpful and polite. This creates a nice atmosphere for one to learn in", another that the experience was "a refreshing change from other prisons".

From the results displayed in *Fig. 6*, it would appear that we were delivering courses in ways which suited the prisoners. Respondents were further asked to specify their preferred learning style. Some ticked more than one box. Fifty-seven per-cent advocated working flexibly with teacher support when required, 43% favoured independent study. Few were in favour of peer support although 31% did welcome traditional teacher-led classroom teaching. Sixty-nine per-cent of respondents answered "yes" to the question, "Are we meeting preferred learning styles", whilst 17% said "no".

With the wide range of skills and educational backgrounds exhibited by the prison population, it would seem that a flexible support system is the most appropriate. Many low skilled prisoner students would feel intimidated by a traditional classroom setting which may remind them of negative experiences from their schooldays. Several respondents commented positively on the value of independent learning. Respondent A in particular was grateful for the opportunity to be trusted to progress at his own pace and Respondent C agreed. Both prisoners were focused, motivated, with clear personal targets and did not require detailed support from teaching staff.

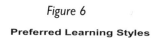

Figure 6

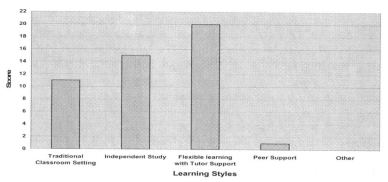

Whilst the above results were gratifying there is never room for complacency. Two respondents, both with previous management experience, provided astute insights into the running of the department. The survey was conducted at a time when education contracts for the region were under renegotiation. Staff were uncertain of their future employment; who they would be working for, under what terms and conditions, indeed whether their employment would continue. Respondent B was disparaging regarding lack of effective communication and poor morale but concluded that "most teaching staff do their best in a poorly managed, under-resourced environment". Respondent D spoke of "insufficient joined-up management which results in delays before decisions are implemented". Both prisoner students were aware of the effect job insecurity was having on staff morale. They witnessed how the department often struggles with "implementing HMP decisions", meeting the requirements of the establishment as well as that of the students.

Conclusions

It is both enlightening and encouraging to see the breadth and variety of qualifications, both non-vocational and vocational, being undertaken by the prisoner students in the establishment concerned, especially when one considers the limitations we face. Prison education has been criticised for offering an 'unremitting diet of basic skills ... unsuitable for many prisoners, but appealing to government because the qualifications are gained fairly quickly and with relative ease' (Steve Taylor of the Forum on Prisoner Education: Press release, January 2005).

Indeed, Key Performance Targets (KPTs), focusing on Basic Skills Entry Level to Level 2, drive prison educators to focus on these qualifications. Non-achievement of the KPTs signifies failure, even if due to offering students a diverse and imaginative curriculum. In this particular department we would appear to be succeeding in striking an acceptable balance for the majority of prisoner students.

In its Annual Report for the year 2004-2005, the Prison Service announces its success at exceeding its own Key Performance Targets. Almost 24,000 awards were achieved at Entry level (target: 15,870); 23,816 at Basic Skills Level 1 (target: 21,890); 14,759 at Level 2 (target: 14,759); and 162,966 Work Skills awards (target: 113,010). Phil Wheatley, Director General of the Prison Service states:

> During 2004-2005 we achieved or exceeded all ten of our targets for resettlement and reducing re-offending, at the same time as improving the quality of most of the programmes that we deliver. We are becoming increasingly successful at getting more prisoners into education and training and into a proper engagement with job centres and all of this improves their chances of getting jobs.

In reply, Steve Taylor, Director of the Forum on Prisoner Education, commented:

> These figures look impressive – and indeed they are. They show how committed and hard-working prison education staff are, and how motivated their students can be. But they don't tell us the levels of need in the prison population; nor do they tell us the number of prisoners who gained A-Level or other higher qualifications. "Death by basic skills" appears set to continue.

One of my respondents echoed this sentiment in his questionnaire, writing: "I don't believe enough attention is paid to the needs of prisoners, unless you have severe reading, writing and numeracy problems".

There are currently no national targets for qualifications above Level 2. In its *Briefing Paper* No. 6, the Forum on Prisoner Education remarks that little research has been undertaken into the educational ability of prisoners at more advanced levels. Only 448 prisoners nationally were registered on OU courses in 2002/3. The Forum argues that:

> Education in prison should be centred on the needs of the individual prisoner. To this end, funding for courses of further and higher education should be increased and made easier to access.

The OLSU aimed to double the number of prisoners undertaking OU degrees by 2005/6. My research supports the view that such targets are feasible. The highest motivation of prisoner-students in my project was the quest for improved knowledge. Yet the question remains – who will fund this commitment? Professor David Wilson argues that:

> It's a damning indictment that of every pound spent on punishment, we spend more than ten pence on security, but less than a penny on education.

Perhaps at the heart of the problem lies the question 'why seek to educate prisoners?' In May 2005, Kevin Warner, Coordinator of Education in the Irish Prison Service, delivered a lecture entitled "Beyond 'Offending Behaviour' – The Wider Perspectives of Adult Education and the European Prison Rules". He outlines the pressures that popular opinion and government authorities place upon prison education departments:

> It is our concern that education, like many other professions and activities in prison, is now expected to give priority attention to the new discourse and its advocacy of programmes that are presumed to address directly the "criminogenic factors" in the prisoner. It would seem to us that the dominance of this discourse has shifted the ground rules. Prison education, like all other activities, must now defend itself primarily in response to the question, how it is addressing offending behaviour? ... As a

result evaluation of prison education tends to be based on whether its courses can be seen to reduce recidivism. (Warner, 2005)

Whilst the paper stresses that 'encouraging and enabling people to turn away for crime to be of the utmost importance', it challenges the 'taken-for-granted assumption that the sole and overriding purpose of prison is to rehabilitate'. Warner welcomes the concept of a broad curriculum, enriching the prisoner-student's existence and enhancing their prospect of personal and intellectual growth. In other words, learning for learning's sake should not be devalued. He suggests an answer to my question:

> We are being asked why and how are we educating prisoners? Perhaps the most common response to the first half of that question from prison educators is that prison education is a moral right that meets a basic human need. This response sees education as a key element of human development. ... The fundamental appeal of a broad curriculum for prison education lies in widening the interests and choices available to the student by providing them with the opportunity to become 'interested in other things'.

One prisoner student who participated in my survey was undertaking a Level 2 Key Skills qualification. As part of the literacy element, he chose to write on the subject of prison education. A short essay he completed is highly critical in particular of the current focus on basic skills and target setting. He felt that skills such as parenting which, in his view were innate, were being "taught, measured and certificated" in order to enhance target figures. He lays blame at the door of these same targets:

> There are two broad views of education. The first is a belief that education is inherently valuable and helps to develop the individual involved. The second holds the view that education should be an activity with measurable hard performance indicators.
>
> Prison education used to be guided by the broader humanistic view. Education departments were sprinkled with classes in politics, current affairs, sociology and the like. Whilst not leading

to any qualifications, save for a few, such classes provided a haven of dignity, humanity and intelligence .... Then "Basic Skills" was introduced (or maybe invented is the right word) and the Social Exclusion Unit proclaimed that prisoners were not qualified for most jobs. The solution was obvious to pull education into the managerialist quicksand and pour resources into producing measurable outcomes.

This response is based on a childish fallacy, making prisoners literate and numerate may be a necessary condition for employment, but it is not a sufficient one. Most employment demands more than the ability to read and write.

The undoubted quality of the above script perhaps illustrates, more eloquently than anything I could say, the intellectual diversity of prisoner students. I have not amended his text in any way, there was no need. He concluded his essay by questioning:

> No targets have been set for GSCEs let alone higher qualifications; is it to be assumed that prisoners are inherently limited to achieving only the most basic levels of literacy and numeracy?

Another open learning student who had an article printed in *Insidetime* (a free monthly newspaper for prisoners) in April 2005 also bitterly condemned this drive to fulfil targets:

> Never make the mistake of imagining that prison education is about you; it is about the contractor meeting targets. You are just a means to that end, and once you have served your purpose then you become a drain.....Prison education abandons us once we reach the level of the average 11-year old. That is the extent of their aspirations for us. God help you if you want to go on to A-level and beyond.

Scathing criticism, and many would say unfair. Contractors must fulfil their obligations to the Prison Service or risk losing that contract. Aspiring to meet the needs of such a diverse population and been able to achieve this within such tight budgetary constrictions is regrettably frequently infeasible. For teaching staff themselves in this environment, this lack of power to help more able prisoner students can be frustrating to say the least.

My small scale study illustrated the sincere commitment of many prisoner students to improve their education. One student, himself a published author, remarked to me: "You either move forward, or stagnate". It is perhaps the students who are more educated prior to their imprisonment who have the 'luxury' of being able to pursue courses from interest rather than necessity. Still more are motivated to gain knowledge and qualifications in the hope of improving their employment prospects on release. Kevin Warner also accepts that the possibility of rehabilitation through education has inestimable value, not just to the prisoner student, but also to society as a whole. A report published by the Prison Reform Trust in 2003 claims that prisoners who do not attend education or training whilst interned are three times more likely to be re-convicted.

Well documented is the financial disincentive many prisoners encounter when hoping to improve their skills by attending full-time education. Whilst pay for full-time prisoner students is usually below £10 per week, between £15 to £30 can often be earned in workshops or other work placements. It is by no means unusual for prisoners to tell you that they 'cannot afford' to attend education.

In an interview for *FE News* in September 2005, Steve Taylor, Director of the Forum on Prisoner Education confirms the significance of this issue:

> One of the big talking points is that if you get paid less for education there's no incentive to learn.... The Government say that there is no evidence that the lower pay [prisoners receive] for education [compared with the pay they get from carrying out chores] prevents some from learning. Well, they only have to talk to prisoners, as the Select Committee did, and they will find evidence of just that. ... What [the Government] often say is that the difference is only a couple of pounds. To a prisoner, whose income is probably about a tenner a week, a couple of pounds is a phone card and another 15 minute conversation with his wife and children.

The main critique of the education department in this survey is not the teaching quality, the diversity of subjects or their delivery; rather our limitations (largely beyond our control) and lack of resources. Whilst many now consider internet use an essential everyday business tool, no prison in England and Wales has controlled internet access for prisoner students. Respondent B told me:

> I understand why (the prison) does not offer email and the internet but feel these areas of education will shortly become mandatory for those who wish to progress in the workplace.

In May 2005, the Forum on Prisoner Education published *Internet Inside*, a report setting out the case for the introduction of internet use for students in prisons. Whilst the internet as a communication and resource tool is increasingly taken for granted by adults and even school children on 'the out', at time of writing very few prisoners have access to this valuable resource. In its Annual Report and Accounts for 2004-5, the Prison Service prioritises 'new learning and skills provision, in line with standards in the community, rolled out from September 2004'. Yet it would seem that this form of provision is being avoided as a political hot potato.

It would be naïve to deny that internet access for prisoners is a thorny and contentious issue. There would of course be requirements for stringent regulations to ensure security and lack of inappropriate use. However, with the blooming of the internet as an essential educational tool, it is uncertain how long the more advanced prisoner student will be able to pursue higher level courses without this option. Indeed, *Internet Inside* quotes a representative of the Open University who, speaking at a conference in October 2004, warned the Director of the OLSU that:

> "If the people studying Open University in prisons do not soon have access to the internet, they won't be able to study with the Open University at all."

To deny prisoner students these valuable opportunities to progress educationally at advanced level would surely be totally unacceptable and unsustainable. In addition to the intellectual benefit and possible future enhancement of career openings, such courses are frequently perceived as a life-line to prisoners. They provide a focus, a goal to aim for, hope for the future. In *Free to Learn?*, Emma Hughes (2004) provides numerous examples of the advantages for distance students and their motivations in undertaking such courses. In the "Students' Experiences" chapter of the pamphlet, the reader's eye is drawn to direct quotes from students participating in her research; quotes such as:

"I've learnt things that I'd never even thought about"

"It gives you an actual purpose"

"Open Uni has shown me I need to take responsibility for my life"

"Education has given me that sense of direction"

"This course actually gave me something to aim for"

Working in prison education, educators themselves have to learn to manage shifts in both internal and national prison policy. Despite such boundaries, the teaching staff in my survey were praised for providing quality support and encouragement in what may be considered a difficult environment. One respondent praises staff as being "polite and caring, along with being encouraging". It would seem that we do meet the needs of *most* prisoner students in our department, yet as stated earlier, there can never be room for complacency. We must continually question how to further improve this provision. Respondent B suggests a possible focus for the future:

> The sole purpose of the education department should be to offer the widest possible variety of vocational training at a level accessible to the majority of prisoners in areas in which there are known significant vacancies as I believe this is the only way in which a significant impact can be made on the current very high cycle of re-offending behaviour.

A challenge indeed. There is no disputing the need of many prison students to gain basic skills in literacy and numeracy. The oft quoted statistics from the Social Exclusion Unit retain their validity. In 2004 the National Audit Office stated:

Whilst 20 per-cent of the general population have basic skills deficiencies, 60 per-cent of prisoners have poor literacy skills and 75 per-cent poor numeracy skills.

However, we must be conscious that these statistics still only represent a *percentage* of the prison population, however sizeable that percentage may be. The remaining 25-40 per-cent of prisoner students have equal rights to further their particular educational needs and skills. This element should not feel abandoned or disenfranchised after reaching the 'holy grail' of Level 2 certificates. If indeed the primary motivation behind prison education is to decrease recidivism and engender rehabilitation, we need to be able to offer offenders more than these basic qualifications and opportunities.

Balancing the differing aims of such a diverse population is a problematic juggling act for any prison education department. Education, when it works, when sincere and effective effort is inputted from both prisoner student and educator, can and does change lives for the better. It must be quality education, targeted at adult individuals, providing structure and purpose on the 'inside' with hope of reintegration on the 'outside' through gained skills, knowledge and qualifications. It must be supported by the Government and Prison Service and link with external agencies. A challenge we must continue to rise to.

Bibliography

Forum on Prisoner Education (2004); Further and Higher Education in Prison. London: Available from: www.fpe.org.uk/filestore/bp06, [Accessed 15.03.2005].

Forum on Prisoner Education (2005); Government must do better on prisoner education. Media release received 07.01.2005 via email.

Her Majesty's Prison Service (2005); Annual Report and Accounts 2004-5. London: www.hmprisonservice.gov.uk/resourcecentre/publicationsdocuments [Accessed 30.10.2005].

Hughes, Emma (2004); Free to Learn? – Prisoner-Students' Views of Distance Learning. Mitcham: Prisoners' Education Trust.

National Audit Office (2004); Youth Offending: The Delivery of Community and Custodial Sentences. London: Office of the Comptroller and Auditor General.

The Offenders' Learning and Skills Unit (2005); Initiatives: Curriculum. London: Department of Education and Skills, Available from: http://www.dfes.gov.uk/ offenderlearning/init_p.cfm?ID=5 [Accessed 14.03.2005].

Prison Reform Trust (2003); Time to Learn: Prisoners' Views on Prison Education. London, Prison Reform Trust.

Social Exclusion Unit (2002); Reducing Reoffending by Ex-Prisoners. London: Office of the Deputy Prime Minister.

Taylor, Steve (2005); Internet Inside. London: Forum on Prisoner Education.

Wilson, David (2004); Speech to Forum on Prisoner Education Evening Reception. London: www.fpe.org.uk [Accessed 20.01.2005].

Wilson, David & Reuss, Anne (Eds.) (2000); Prison(er) Education - Stories of Change and Transformation. Winchester: Waterside Press.

PRIME: Prison Media

Barbara Schofield

Choppa has scarcely sat at a computer before. Now, wearing head-phones, and gazing intently at the screen in front of him, he is manipulating digital blocks of audio and moving them around the screen; working with voices, music and sound effects in a multi- track editing system called 'CoolEdit'. This is how they do it at BBC Radio Five Live and at the *Today* programme on Radio 4. He is absorbed in his new-found skills for a while and then turns to the tutor with a smile, flashing a galaxy of gold capped teeth, "This is a long way from armed robbery!" He is serving nearly five years for violent crime and has been in and out of prison since he was 15. He describes himself as "a criminal with a brain".

Choppa is one of a cohort of fifteen students working towards a nationally recognised qualification, the BTEC National Award in Radio at HMP Wandsworth, a large local prison in south-west London. What was once a large hall at the end of 'D' Wing full of industrial sewing machines has been converted into a workshop and education area. At one end, properly sound proofed, a fully equipped radio studio complex with a 'talk studio' and a couple of control rooms have been built. Next to the studios, a spacious classroom is equipped with computers with CoolEdit, which link directly to the control desk computer in the radio studio.

Wandsworth is not the first prison to recognise the value of radio to a captive audience of whom a third have a reading age of eleven or less. Add to that the problem of communication within a sizeable community of nearly 1500 prisoners and more than three hundred prison officers, and running a prison radio station begins to appear a cost effective and user friendly solution. HMP Wandsworth is however the first to combine the effective running of a small-scale, low powered radio station - the signal ends at the prison walls - with an on-going training programme in radio production skills, delivered by an external education provider and linked to a comprehensive support and outreach programme for students after release.

This model of prison radio has been formulated by the UK-based educational media consultancy, Radio for Development (RFD). Before this, RFD worked entirely in developing countries, using the cost-effective, accessible and flexible medium of radio to support a wide range of public education campaigns, including malaria prevention programmes with the World Health Organisation in sub-Saharan Africa and civic education projects with local partners in the South Pacific Islands. To date, RFD has worked in over 30 countries around the world, and its Director, James Greenshields, sees obvious and interesting parallels:

> I was reading an article about prison education in a national newspaper and realised that exactly the same sense of isolation and lack of access to a broad range of educational opportunity applies to prisoners in the UK as to communities in the developing world. For people who are disempowered and have low literacy rates, radio can be a way back into education and to taking control of your own life. We've found broadcasting with a strong interactive element fits well into prison life – prisoners welcome having a voice and want to air their views, not just on conditions in the jail but on the wider world, and through poetry, drama, comedy, radio soap opera and via all sorts of talents.

The Prison Radio Project was launched in January 2004 by Cherie Booth QC, and the then Prisons and Probation Minister Paul Goggins MP. Both Mr Goggins and the former Shadow Prisons Minister, Cheryl Gillan MP have visited the studios and been interviewed by students, who even-handedly gave each of them a Jeremy Paxman-style grilling about prison and its effectiveness. The in-house radio station is named 'Radio Wanno', after the not-quite-affectionate way the prison is referred to by its occupants. Its output is largely determined by the students themselves, but the underlying theme is that whatever is produced and broadcast has relevance for the 'prison community', which includes governors, officers, and those working for the many agencies which operate within the prison walls. So when Gavin produces a short radio item about missing his baby daughter and tries to work out how he can still be a good dad and role model, the piece connects to information about the 'Family Man' and 'Fathers Inside' classes being offered at Wandsworth. This may link to details of how to book a special family visiting on a Sunday, when toys and mats brought into the visiting hall, for dads to do some hands-on parenting with their children.

Of course, setting up a radio station in a prison – especially a prison like Wandsworth – was not an easy task. The prison is a typical Victorian gaol, with five wings radiating from the centre. Each wing in turn houses prisoners on four levels or landings. Installing the induction loop which would carry a reliable radio signal to all levels of the prison was not the easiest of tasks, and initially reception to some wings and landings was patchy. There was also understandable reluctance on the part of the governor and senior management to allow any live broadcasting, even by trusted prisoners, which has meant a commitment to producing content in entirely pre-recorded form. The turnover of prisoners in Wandsworth, as a local prison with a high percentage of men on remand or awaiting sentencing, is high, which has meant retaining students long enough for them to gain the qualification has sometimes been problematic. In addition, there was an early expectation among some prison staff and from some prisoners that the radio station output would be music-based and that the impact of the project would be low-level and relatively limited. It was instructive to see how this perception changed as the radio training and broadcasting began to make an impact on life and procedures within the prison. Recognising this, from January 2005 the prison has been funding management of the project under the terms of a service level agreement, at the point when initial charitable trust funding through the Paul Hamlyn Foundation was coming to an end.

The promise that education and training would be central to the radio project meant that governors, education managers and voluntary agencies within the prison were strongly supportive right from the start. It also became apparent early on that having prisoners equipped with the skills and training to produce sophisticated media products, with an emphasis on speech-based radio output, could have a beneficial effect on the flow of communication within the prison. A significant inroad into existing practices within the prison was made when the project, with the full support of the governor and senior staff, accepted student prisoners from both the main wing of the prison and from the normally entirely separate Vulnerable Prisoners' Unit and trained them alongside each other. So from the outset the project had at its core a sense of innovation and integration, the idea that prisoners of all types and all backgrounds were entirely capable of learning and working together with a common cause and sense of purpose. Also underpinning this model was the belief that a 'joined up' approach to learning, which linked it with responsible and worthwhile endeavour ('work') inside the prison and with support on resettlement would benefit prison and prisoner alike.

HMP Wandsworth's former education manager, Trish Smith, was instrumental in establishing the project within the prison, and her successor, Judy Fitt, is equally supportive:

> What really appealed about the radio project was the concentration on learning practical and relevant skills which didn't discriminate against non-traditional learners. We also welcomed the idea that prisoners would have a properly equipped radio studio of exactly the type they would find on the outside, and that the training they did in prison might help them find worthwhile employment opportunities on release. The training course has become one of the most popular and over subscribed in the prison because prisoners can see they are learning skills and techniques in an environment which is as far as possible a replication of a real work situation.

The qualification at the core of the project at HMP Wandsworth is the BTEC National Award in Radio, delivered initially by Lambeth College and more recently by the London Metropolitan University. There are several compelling reasons why this qualification is more likely to engage those who for whatever reason have been discouraged or disaffected by experiences of school and learning. It is believed that four out of five prisoners typically exhibit writing skills at or below the level expected of an eleven year-old. For most prisoners then, the emphasis on practically based modules within the BTEC course is a real advantage. Choppa and his fellow students can work on programmes for assessment at the computer, using CoolEdit and submitting their work in audio form, as a CD or minidisk for tutors and external examiners to mark. A substantial part of the work for the BTEC (Radio) consists of a half hour long radio programme, the Final Major Project. Among the first cohort of Wandsworth radio students were two students with severe dyslexia. The BTEC allows such students to submit assignments in a non printed form – through video or voice recording – and if necessary a 'scribe' can be assigned to do their typing. This method of learning and assessment clearly suits the non-traditional learner far better than the conventional demands of an 'A' Level – to which the BTEC is an equivalent – with its emphasis on essays and written coursework.

Students in prison also appreciate and respond to the areas of choice offered by the BTEC Award, choosing from a range of modules which include interviewing and presentational techniques, devising a radio drama and producing it for broadcast, or the production of a short piece of radio with more than one voice or opinion known in the broadcasting industry as a 'radio package'. The BTEC also offers a news module if students and tutors want to consider adding a journalistic slant to the learning programme. For those who are disempowered in virtually every other aspect of their everyday lives, the notion of choice – even if all students in one cohort need to choose the same set of options – is an appealing one. Indeed, the process of choosing a set of modules which everyone agrees on is generally an object lesson in negotiation, interpersonal and team-working skills. At HMP Wandsworth, tutors have found students are strongly inclined towards the freedom of thought and creativity offered by the drama module. Kris, aged 32, has done some acting on the outside, but had never considered trying his skills in writing drama. He devised an artful, intricate radio series with as many twists and turns as your average edition of *EastEnders*. The only difference here was that the cast, instead of being market stallholders or the landlady of the 'Queen Vic', was drawn from the multitude of feral pigeons which hang around the yards, roofs and buildings of the prison. He was struck by the petty squabbling and sexual competitiveness among the birds, which was what set him off with his radio series:

> I used to watch the birds from my window and after a while I could pick out particular ones, and certain ways they behaved. I realised that they were all competing for food, for sexual favours, for space, for the room to ruffle their feathers and make a show in front of the other pigeons. Instead of writing about life in here, I thought I'd showcase the activities of the pigeons – and when I thought about it they were doing all the same things we're all doing inside – and try and make it funny as well as having a serious side.

After this inspired imaginative leap, Kris had to work on finding the right sound effects, casting actors to fulfil all the roles, writing a script which was accessible to every prisoner, and recording the contributions in the studio. This kind of multi-layered endeavour demands interpersonal, creative and logistical skills at a quite sophisticated and demanding level. All this had to happen before he could sit down and edit the final production to a given time and format using fine motor skills and endless patience to get the result he wanted. Encouraged by the success of his radio series, Kris next turned his hand to a dramatic exposition of the events which led to the trial, conviction and subsequent hanging in Wandsworth Prison of Derek Bentley, the last man to go to the gallows at the prison.

The emphasis on flexibility and combining skills in a practical setting tends to bring out dormant enthusiasm and determination in prisoners who long ago gave up on more conventionally delivered education of the 'paper and pen' variety. "I've found something I can do" declares Dwayne, closing the microphone faders after producing a radio interview with the governor which combines sensitivity with hardnosed questioning. "I've found something I want to do", he adds as an afterthought. London Metropolitan University is currently delivering the BTEC programme at HMP Wandsworth and intends to be part of the expansion of the project to other prisons. As Professor John Gabriel, Head of the Department of Applied Social Sciences explains, the move into media production training within prisons fits perfectly with the University's acknowledged aims:

> It addresses our main mission objective which is to engage with hard-to-reach and socially excluded groups. In common with some other new Universities we attract students from a wide range of backgrounds and we're interested in working with students whose progression through the education system has not been smooth. We'd already done research on the prison sector and believed it was an area we could contribute to. Also, this Department [of Applied Social Sciences] has an exceptionally strong media area and we were interested in working around and expanding in the area of media production.

With the exception of 'Scrubs' [HMP Wormwood Scrubs] I've spent time in every London jail. My last was in Wanno where I spent nine months. I was right there at the beginning of the radio project and I can tell you many of the staff and inmates saw it as a bit of a joke – 'summink for the DJs' they said. Truth be told I reckon many didn't think inmates had the brain capacity to learn anything like that. But now they've seen what it can achieve they've had to eat their words. What they forget is that prisoners are simply products of the environment in which they live and they are just as smart as the next person.   (Mark, a Radio Wanno student, now studying on a degree course in Media and Communications at Goldsmiths College, University of London.)

Many prisoners have come from chaotic backgrounds and families and have had no opportunity or inclination to develop patterns of responsible behaviour which take other people's needs and feelings into account. While the qualification encourages self-expression through drama, poetry and creative script writing on a very individual basis, Kamal Prashar, the Course Leader at Wandsworth, believes one of the many advantages of the BTEC is that it fosters both self-esteem and more responsible patterns of behaviour:

> Much of the course requires students to work in groups of various sizes and contribute towards ideas development, management of assignments and organisation to ensure that deadlines are achieved. By working in groups the students are often being exposed to difficult situations and having to overcome these democratically which shows the non-specific benefits of the course. As well as team working assignments the students are also given individual assignments and in these they have to show their self management and creative skills to develop and complete tasks, often with tutors acting in a purely advisory role once the tasks have been set. The increase in self worth that can result from such an experience cannot be measured but the change in confidence and communication skills as well as trouble shooting and forward planning is demonstrable after even just a few weeks.

Students also appreciate the variety of learning and assessment offered within the BTEC course. Work for assessment can be produced in written, audio, presentation-based, survey or research data form or a combination of these. Accumulating this range of skills offers clear vocational advantages for prisoners on release. Because of the number and diversity of radio stations in Greater London and the South-East, most prisoners in London's prisons are very conscious of the opportunities in community radio and restricted short licence broadcasting. Some have already tried their hand at broadcasting, legally or otherwise, or have a qualification in sound recording or sound engineering. No-one is pretending that, on release, they will all walk into radio presenter jobs at 'Choice FM' or become late-night DJs on one of the many music-based stations operating in and around London, but the increase in confidence and interpersonal skills they are developing through, for example, learning how to conduct a radio round-table debate with several guests, may make a difference to their job prospects.

There is also a wider vocational potential. A whole range of vocational opportunities is opened up by the radio training and the two core modules in Research Techniques and Production Management which all students have to undertake; work in media-based projects, advertising and commercial production houses, music production companies, press offices, opportunities in digital communications, market and consumer research organisations among many others. Successful students – and success rates at Wandsworth had been above the national average for the qualification, with many gaining high grades – can show potential employers a portfolio demonstrating evidence of ability to multi-task, to work both in a team and flexibly on their own initiative, combined with the ability to plan and organise in the longer term and to work to a deadline, as Kamal Prashar explains:

> We may ultimately be preparing people for a career in radio but clearly far more than that is happening. Doing this course is helping people to find out who they really are, how they work under pressure, how they achieve a sense of self worth and how they communicate often complex ideas to others in such a way that they understand. Radio production teaches people how to be confident and able to speak for themselves and although my own evidence may be anecdotal, it does seem that inmates need to be able to do this if they are going to value their abilities and make the first steps to a life without re-offending.

The most compelling reason previously disaffected prisoners are flocking to enrol on the course is that they enjoy listening to radio and consider it an important part of their lives. Virtually every prisoner has a radio and/or television in his cell and most watch and listen avidly, discussing programmes and output with friends, officers and cellmates. Every newspaper that comes into the prison is passed around the landings and cells and therefore read by dozens of people. Prisoners care what is going on in the outside world and have an opinion on current events. Most prisoners are critical and sophisticated consumers and have a well-developed appreciation of mass media and its importance in the world. This highly developed interest and awareness makes media training completely relevant to learners who may long since have turned away from forms of learning which they consider irrelevant. As Choppa explains:

> I'd never put myself forward for education before, because I thought it was nothing to do with me, nothing I could do. But when I heard my programme on the radio, when my friends on the wing heard a vox-pop I did with them, I felt proud of what I could do. I could feel myself getting more confident with other things as well. I calmed down a lot once I was doing the radio training, and instead of shouting or arguing with other inmates sometimes like I used to, I just walked away. The radio thing has made me feel bigger and better about myself and my abilities.

It is a view shared by Professor John Gabriel from London Metropolitan University:

> The media is something prisoners and other disadvantaged groups can relate to. It's not an abstraction. It's a great vehicle for engaging learners. People who are not necessarily signed up for education are avidly listening to radio, watching television, reading newspapers. It's about connecting with people through their interests. I also believe that having a practical element, getting people to do things, enhances learning and critical thinking. Participation is very important to the whole process.

This pioneering model at HMP Wandsworth includes a comprehensive package of support to prisoners during the course, over the remainder of their time in prison, and, crucially, on release. Not finding work or having any prospect of employment is a significant factor in the well-trodden cycle of conviction, release and re-offending. Fewer than one in three of the 90,000 people who leave prison every year have a job or an educational or training place to go to. The Prison Radio Outreach Project (PROP) works alongside students in working out their personal ambitions for training and employment, whilst dealing with any substance misuse or housing issues they might have. Each student receives vital information and signposting towards support structures in the South East of England through The PROP Handbook. This unique 'toolkit' of information and contacts is divided into six sections: Education & Training; Employment; Health; Housing; Grants & Benefits; and Within Prison. The use of the Handbook is supported through regular one-to-one sessions with PROP's welfare worker, combined with group workshops led by resettlement experts from partner organisations.

PROP's mentoring programme offers support on release to graduates of the training programme. Many of the mentors are prominent journalists or broadcast producers or presenters from either BBC or commercial radio and television. Some are established playwrights or television actors. The support they provide ranges from helping with practical issues like putting together an attractive curriculum vitae to giving intensive support over the period following release. PROP's links with partner organisations mean students have realistic and wider-ranging options for the future, both within and outside the media sector. These include opportunities such as a business start-up packages, work in the voluntary sector, degree courses or vocational training. One of PROP's strongest partnerships is with the 'Open Book' project at the University of London's Goldsmiths College, a project that supports ex-offenders into degree programmes. So far, four graduates of the Wandsworth course have taken up degree courses at the College, including Kris, who is studying for a BA in Drama and Theatre Studies.

The role of PROP, which has been financially supported by the Esmée Fairbairn Foundation, is one which will be increasingly absorbed by the facilities and structures of London Metropolitan University, as Professor John Gabriel from London Metropolitan University explains:

> This is an important and significant area which we want to address. People with criminal records face a further barrier when looking for employment. We can think of ways of tapping into the resources we have here at the University – the careers services for instance. And our databases and employer forums can be used to explore the strong links with employers we have developed, to the benefit of those with a record of convictions. There are ways we can expand on the excellent mentoring scheme PROP has developed, and we can build direct links to some of our courses for those who want to continue studying when they leave prison.

While Radio Wanno plays a leading role in broadcasting accessible information and advice on a daily basis throughout HMP Wandsworth, once the project was established, governors and senior managers suggested that certain crucial procedures – notably Induction and Resettlement – would benefit from additional targeted support. It is well documented that prisoners arriving in custody are at their most vulnerable and that these first few weeks are when a newly-arrived prisoner is most likely to attempt suicide. However well intentioned, prison officers are hard pressed simply processing new arrivals – almost 4000 prisoners pass through Wandsworth prison every year – and with the prison at bursting point there is little opportunity to reassure or counsel new prisoners. In May 2004 therefore an English-language Induction CD was produced, narrated by a serving prisoner and offering user-friendly, prisoner to prisoner advice and information on key areas such as how to organise phone calls and visits from family and friends, how to get help getting off drugs or alcohol, and how to get the support of a Listener (a prisoner trained by the Samaritans). This is currently issued to each new prisoner along with a portable CD player, which he returns once he has taken in the information in his cell in his own time. Versions in Arabic, French, Spanish and Urdu – the most common languages spoken at Wandsworth – are at the planning stage.

This initiative was picked up by the National Institute for Adult Continuing Education (NIACE) which commissioned RFD's team to produce similarly user-friendly and accessible information in CD form as part of the re-branding of 'Basic Skills' to 'Skills for Life'. Project team members worked in five prisons, including Wandsworth, recording both male and female prisoners' educational experiences and aspirations and focusing on opportunities for learning which prisoners can access. These were issued to education departments in all prisons in England and Wales, in different versions for the male and female estates, and are being used to encourage and support the take-up of courses and classes. These are narrated by serving or recently released prisoners, and offer encouraging personal histories from prisoners who, until they enrolled on education courses in prison, believed they were no-hopers, beyond the reach of learning.

Because I left school without taking any qualifications whatsoever, I always thought of myself as really a bit of a thickie. Now I know that I'm very intelligent and I'm putting it to good use. The more I learn the more I want to learn.

I've been in prison now over 9 and a half years. When I was training and getting qualifications I felt that I was getting something out of the prison for myself rather than just being a prison number going through a sentence.

Caz and Mia, interviewed at HMP Foston Hall in Derbyshire for the 'Skills for Life' CD

Tackling public attitudes to crime and punishment has been a priority of the Prison Radio Project from the start. There has been enormous media interest in the 'radio station run by prisoners inside prison' especially with the emphasis on reflective programming which highlights education and training opportunities in the prison, offers crucial advice and information to prisoners in a number of languages, and showcases the great variety of talent and creativity among Wandsworth prisoners. Several graduates of the BTEC course have appeared on national and local radio, dispelling many myths about prisons and prisoners, and helping to normalise public perceptions of those with a criminal record as inarticulate and anti-social. The Schools Outreach Project, which was piloted in April 2004, is an extension of this approach specifically targeted at schools and youth groups. Prison Media graduates are given the opportunity to use their enhanced communication skills to present their experiences of life before, during and after their sentence. These presentations also make use of materials produced within the prison in order to reflect the realities of life behind bars in a vivid and engaging way, whilst allowing teenagers to explore the issues that can lead to imprisonment. Jonathon was among the first BTEC graduates to undertake this work at a youth group in Wandsworth:

I told them what being in jail was really like – that it's not a good place to be. Kids are inquisitive, they wanted to know all sorts. 'What's the food like', 'How much time do you get out of your cell' 'Do you get a TV or a computer?' It was good, we had a laugh but they got the message. I've spent too much time in prison and I told them it's not the way to go.

Another way of reaching this age group – Key Stage 3 and 4 students – is being devised through an on-line project linking into the citizenship curriculum, being formulated with the backing of the Department for Culture, Media and Sport's 'Culture Online' programme. Focusing on an interactive website, this project will explore a wide cross-section of issues within the criminal justice sector, using a state of the art combination of video footage, audio material, and graphic design. Highly innovative elements of the project will include the input of audio/visual materials from prisoners, as well as compelling testimonies from victims of crime. The project will be specifically targeted towards teachers and students of citizenship, within both schools and youth groups. Online educational resource materials will assist teachers in the delivery of a sensitive but highly relevant subject.

The model of Prison Radio which has worked so well at Wandsworth is to be replicated on a much expanded scale within the female prison estate. HMP Downview in Surrey is to be the base for a major media training and production centre which will offer radio, television/video and desk-top publishing training courses lasting between three and six months. During this time the students will be actively contributing to the output of an in-house radio station, as at Wandsworth, but also to the in-cell television output within the prison, and to the publication of a regular newsletter. In-cell television output will have a particular emphasis on supporting the Induction and Resettlement procedures and processes at Downview. These activities will essentially be inward looking, serving the prison and the informational needs of the prison community. All Downview trainees will additionally have access to the London Metropolitan University's resource, the Women's Library, as a research centre. This is especially relevant as internet access, as in virtually all prisons, is limited or denied. Alongside the training, however, Downview will become the focus of a multi-media Production Centre providing professionally produced media products. With the emphasis on the production of high-quality accessible information in the prisoner to prisoner format which has worked so well at Wandsworth, the project is now being re-named and re-focussed as PRIME – Prison Media.

Downview's Production Centre will operate as a social enterprise along well-defined business principles, producing audio, video and print materials for prisons within London & the South East, as well as voluntary sector agencies operating within the criminal justice system. The emphasis will be on participating prisoners learning sound marketing, advertising, distributive, organisational and stocktaking skills which will in turn attract a nationally-recognised qualification. These women will be graduates of the core qualification in radio, television/video or desktop publishing. Depending on their sentences, they can either choose to work on the in-house radio or television station or produce the prisoner-led newsletter, or they can progress to working within the Production Centre towards specially commissioned media products. All participating prisoners will be able to take advantage of support towards further training or employment already offered by PROP at Wandsworth.

Working at HMP Wandsworth has demonstrated to the Project team the pressing need for accessible and user-friendly information and communications materials within a prison. Officers are generally too hard-pressed to spend time on a one-to-one basis explaining the ins and outs of daily life to new prisoners, or to support individual prisoners coming up to release and making difficult decisions about their future. Many prison officers do a fantastic and largely unsung job in this area, as do the specific agencies which work in prisons. Providing prisoners themselves with the skills and technology to fill the information gap in a flexible and responsive way, while gaining important and relevant vocational skills, makes clear sense for prison management, officers and prisoners. At the same time, media products themselves can be produced so that each reinforces the other.

For instance, the Production Centre may be commissioned to produce a video for use with groups of women prisoners who have been convicted for drug importation. This could be used to spark off a discussion facilitated by a specially trained counsellor, psychologist or welfare worker on how to get out of the cycle which convinced them to take such a step, often leaving dependent children at home. On the back of this, participating women may be given printed information – which could be produced in several different languages -- to take away from the group. In each case, materials will have been produced by prisoners working directly with women in this position, and will be jargon-free and without the stamp of 'officialdom'.

Radio For Development's Director, James Greenshields, believes that PRIME at Downview will become a template for a network of similar prison-based media centres across England, with set-up costs funded through the National Offender Management Service (NOMS) but rapidly becoming financially autonomous through the model of an income-generating social enterprise.

In this model education is the vehicle for rehabilitation. PRIME offers real opportunities for prisoners to undertake training and work within prisons which makes such sense to them. And with support, they'll be able to offer these very marketable skills to employers on the outside. Media is central to all our lives and prisoners are no different. And the real beneficiary is the prison itself – when prisoners are kept properly informed -- on drug rehab programmes, on when the visit to the gym is, on how to get a Halal meal – there's less hassle in the prison which means the whole establishment will work better and be a more productive place for everyone.

Educational, Vocational and 'Thinking Skills' Provision in HM Prisons

Jill Clark, Ian Hall & David Moseley

Introduction

The survey is the first phase of a research project funded by the Learning and Skills Development Agency (LSDA) which is evaluating the impact of English Speaking Board (ESB) communication courses in prisons in England and Wales. The purpose of this study is 'to build a picture of the delivery of interventions which seek to improve the thinking skills of prisoners' and thereby to contextualise the ESB courses in oral communication. The present research team saw an opportunity to carry out an independent evaluation of the ESB approach, both retrospectively and prospectively. The prima facie evidence was that ESB oral communication courses are emotionally powerful for many and may well bring other benefits, even perhaps reducing recidivism by opening up alternative paths, including employment options. The opportunity to immediately transfer oral communication skills to other contexts (including other courses) within and outside prisons is always available to prisoners, whereas this applies much less with other kinds of course.

The research project was planned as follows:

(1) A postal survey carried out in prisons in England and Wales to ascertain which courses are believed by prison staff to help develop thinking skills;

(2) A retrospective study to evaluate the impact on recidivism of taking an ESB oral communication course during the period of the Lottery-funded project 1999-2002;

(3) A prospective experimental study was planned to test the hypothesis that, after successfully completing ESB courses, prisoners are able to communicate better with fellow prisoners and prison staff; and

(4) Four case studies, using largely qualitative methods, to compare different approaches to the development of thinking skills.

It is the first phase of our research, the postal questionnaire survey, which is the focus of this article. Before exploring these findings it is important to set out the policy context within which this study is taking place.

The Political Climate

The prison service as we know it today is based on two functions: imprisonment and punishment of prisoners (and therefore protection of the public) and the provision of activities to educate and rehabilitate, and therefore reduce re-offending. The rehabilitation of offenders has been the subject of several reports and policy changes during the last few years. For example, in 2001 a report on Resettlement by HM Inspectors of Prisons (2001) recommended improved joint working between prisons and probation, and concluded that although three-quarters of initial sentence plans contained targets to address offending behaviour, risk and other needs, the research showed that only about a third were judged to have done this 'satisfactorily', or 'well'. On offender behaviour provision generally, the report found that: 'although the provision of accredited and non-accredited programmes was widespread in prison, a strategic approach had not been developed, and too many offenders were leaving prison without their offending behaviour having been addressed' (HMI Prisons, 2001).

Early in 2002, the National Audit Office (with the Prison Service) concluded that the Service needed to make certain that all offenders who would benefit from attending programmes whilst in prison do so and that 'many prisoners leave prison without having had the opportunity to address their offending behaviour' (NAO, 2002). Later in that same year, British Prime Minister, Tony Blair, admitted that although crime was down 21% since 1997, there was still a long way to go in relation to re-offending by ex-prisoners:

People who have been in prison account for one in five of all crimes. Nearly three in five prisoners are re-convicted within two years of leaving prison. Offending by ex-prisoners costs society at least £11 billion a year. This all tells us we are failing to capitalise on the opportunity prison provides to stop people offending for good (Blair, Foreword, Social Exclusion Unit (SEU) 2002:3).

Recommendations from the SEU report included the development of a National Rehabilitation Strategy. A further parallel report, *Managing Offenders, Reducing Crime* (Carter, 2003), was produced as a result of a correctional services review - which also suggested the need for a more 'joined up' approach to working - concluded that the system remains dominated by the need to administer both the prison and probation service rather than focus on the offender and reducing re-offending. A solution to this, Carter proposed, was to develop the National Offender Management Service (NOMS), which should restructure the current activities of prison *and* probation to provide 'end-to-end' management of offenders who receive either a community or custodial sentence.

Alongside these reviews and suggestions for change, the Criminal Justice Act 2003, for the first time, laid down the *purposes* of sentencing for courts, which includes a reference to rehabilitation:

- The punishment of offenders
- The reduction of crime, including its reduction by deterrence
- The reform and rehabilitation of offenders
- The protection of the public, and
- The making of reparation by offenders to persons affected by their offences.
(taken from Home Office, 2004c).

Taking the work and recommendations of the Carter report further, *Reducing Crime – Changing Lives* (2004) documented the next strategy of the Government to improve the effectiveness of the criminal justice system, and more specifically, the correctional services. Increased emphasis is now on co-ordinated programmes of work, training and education for individual prisoners in order to make a significant difference to prisoner's life chances and rates of re-offending and re-conviction.

The recent National Action Plan, *Reducing Reoffending* (Home Office 2004b; 2004c) is a result of all these preceding documents, and outlines the Government's plans to reduce reoffending through strategic direction and joined-up working. At the centre of the plan, NOMS aims to bring together prisons and probation and help to develop an effective case management approach. The document also takes forward two important Government manifesto commitments:

- to ensure that punishment and rehabilitation are both designed to minimise re-offending;
- and to improve the education of those offenders in custody (Home Office 2004b).

Given that the prison population currently stands at an all time high of 75,203 (as at 03/12/04) and is continuing to rise (the total population at the time of our questionnaire survey - 15/04/02 - was 73,012), such political interest and strategic changes are clearly timely. Despite this increased population, it is clear that progress towards targets is good, with the provision of basic skills training a priority. In 2002-3, in basic skills qualifications, there were 9,179 at entry level compared to a target of 6,000. There were 16,989 qualifications at Level 1 compared to a target of 12,000 and there were 15,145 qualifications at Level 2 compared to a target of 10,800. This gives a total outturn of 41,313 Basic Skills awards compared to an overall target of 28,800. The national target for Key Work Skills was exceeded by an even more substantial margin. There were 89,201 qualifications delivered against a national target of 45,000, which is almost double (HM Prison Service, 2003). The report concludes that it is important that prisons continue to:

> ... deliver against these targets, both as a contribution to improving the basic skills of adults in the population, and as a means of reducing the likelihood of individuals re-offending. But it is equally important that prisons deliver education and training of a high quality which is relevant to the needs of individuals, and which will equip them with skills they need to lead useful lives when they return to the community (HM Prison Service, 2003).

In addition to the policy changes and implementation plans, there have been changes in relation to the funding of education and training of offenders. Following the 2002 Spending Review settlement, the funding for education and training of prisoners increased to £97 million in 2003-2004, £122 million in 2004-2005 and £137 million in 2005-2006. This will bring about substantial increases in the volume of education and training in prisons and will also provide resources for further innovation and quality improvement. Part of the funding has been used to appoint Heads of Learning and Skills across the prisons estate, who will oversee the development of education and training in all parts of their respective establishments.

Other key development are the expansion of the Offenders' Learning and Skills Unit's (OLSU) remit from 2004-2005 to cover education and training for offenders who are serving sentences in the community, and (in conjunction with the Learning and Skills Council) the development and regional testing of elements of the Offenders' Learning and Skills Service (OLASS). These developments will bring new opportunities for aligning the provision that is offered to offenders on probation with that available in prisons, and for improving continuity of learning opportunities. While focus has been on basic skills and vocational qualifications, the Prison Service has continued to deliver offending behaviour courses, albeit in smaller numbers.

Prisoners and Learning

There is a view that prison experience is in itself a damaging experience – both practically and emotionally (see, for example, Worrall, 2004). On a practical level, prisoners are likely to suffer from a loss of housing, employment and family contact. Emotionally, institutionalisation can lead to few opportunities to make decisions or take responsibility for their own actions. Education in prison, therefore, is regarded as a tool for mitigating such damage, and for over a hundred years prison systems on both sides of the Atlantic have been developing prisoner programmes that aim to rehabilitate prisoners into society. The learning processes involved have been seen as valuable both for the individuals concerned and for society as a whole. Yet research and policy has concentrated on attempts to change individuals rather than on attempts to deal with the strongly linked societal factors of crime and unemployment simultaneously.

Different prison education programmes have different purposes and draw upon different branches of applied psychology and pedagogical approaches in different ways and to differing degrees. There are, for example:

- vocational programmes which aim to improve prisoners' employment prospects;
- ICT programmes which aim to develop awareness and use of new technology;
- basic skills programmes;
- literacy for lifelong learning;
- personal development programmes which aim to modify/develop prisoners' thinking/ behaviour (sometimes referred to as general offending behaviour programmes and cognitive skills programmes);
- programmes based around the humanities which aim to cultivate individual critical and creative abilities through a broad liberal curriculum; and
- faith-based programmes which aim to promote a set of religious values and beliefs and associated behaviours.

These involve different approaches to teaching and learning and different ideas about how knowledge and identity are constructed. They may emphasise:

- individual/ isolated learning;
- teacher-led or 'direct' instruction;
- mastery learning of skills built up from their components;
- knowledge acquisition based on reading/writing/oracy/multimedia;
- the development of practical skills through modelling and guided practice;
- student-centred learning with the teacher as a facilitator of meaning-making;
- problem solving drawing on personal experience and meeting real-life needs;
- language and discourse development through dialogue in groups;
- the examination of ideas, beliefs and values through Socratic questioning; and
- critical thinking, reflection and transformative learning.

The article by Wilson *et al* (2000) provides an excellent discussion of a meta-analysis of American correction-based education, vocation, and work programs for adult offenders. The article is based on research which compared 33 independent experimental evaluations of education, vocation and work programs and found that program participants reoffend at a lower rate than non-participants. The study itself recommends that future evaluative research could be strengthened through the incorporation of theoretical links between program activities and future criminal involvement and through designs that control for self-selection bias beyond basic demographic differences.

However, it is not just psychological personal development programmes that are thought to reduce reoffending: vocational and educational programmes can be equally if not more effective. Pawson (2000) suggested that the rehabilitative outcome of prisoner education stems from improved competence (including social skills and reflection). Educational experiences can help build character and raise self-confidence and aspirations. Pawson summarised the benefits of the Simon Fraser Prison Education Programme in Canada where 654 participants had a reoffending rate of 25% instead of a predicted 42% (a massive 40% improvement). He also addressed the important issues of why the programme was effective, for whom, in what circumstances and in what respects.

Prison as a learning environment is a unique location to say the least. The students can have a variety of abilities and prior experience, attendance is not always voluntary, and motivations for attending may be extrinsic rather than intrinsic. It should be noted that earlier in their lives many prisoners may have been excluded from school for this kind of behaviour. In the UK it is reported that prisoners are over twenty times more likely than the general population to have been excluded from school and ten times as likely to have truanted regularly (SEU, 2002). Others have simply dropped out and have been drawn into crime through the influence of gangs and drug dealers (*ibid.*).

Prisoners are rarely equipped with the skills which are valued by employers, and prominent amongst these are oral communication and interpersonal skills (Hall *et al.*, 1999). The National Employers Skills Survey carried out in 2003 again yielded the same findings, drawing attention to a lack of motivation on the part of employees as the second most common reason for skill deficits (Hogarth et al., 2004).

Very little is known about the communicative competence of prisoners on entry to prison and we know of no research on the issue. Minority ethnic groups make up 18% of the male and 25% of the female prison population and 8% of the prison population are foreign nationals. It is not unusual for prison inspection reports to draw attention to the need to provide more support for prisoners who do not understand English. However, there is reason to believe that verbal communication skills are a common area of weakness irrespective of language background.

Thinking Skills Interventions in Prisons

Thinking skills interventions in schools, colleges and universities are typically designed to improve educational outcomes, especially through developing critical and creative thinking and enabling learners to regulate their thinking and learning more effectively. Moseley and colleagues (2004) define thinking skills approaches as 'courses or organised activities which identify for learners translatable mental processes and/or which require learners to plan, describe and evaluate their thinking and learning'. The long-term aim of such courses is to improve strategic thinking, self-awareness and reflection together with a positive set of values, beliefs and personal qualities.

The thinking skills (or cognitive skills) interventions developed specifically for use in prisons have been strongly influenced by developments in clinical psychology, especially the development and use of cognitive behaviour therapies. Unlike thinking skills interventions with an educational focus, they are primarily directed at changing patterns of behaviour. Nonetheless, the generic characterisation of thinking skills approaches used by Moseley and colleagues in their report to the LSDA (2004) also applies to these programmes. In England and Wales, thinking skills interventions in prisons (usually known as Offending Behaviour Programmes, or OBPs) are generally organised and delivered through prison psychology departments and do not fall under the remit of either Education Managers or Heads of Learning and Skills. The staff involved are mainly psychologists and prison or probation officers, but may include people with educational training and experience who have trained as tutors.

First introduced into HM Prison Service in 1992, the principal aim of the Offending Behaviour Programmes is to reduce the likelihood of reoffending. Secondary aims are to improve behaviour, problem solving skills, and attitudes. The most well-developed and popular of these is the Reasoning and Rehabilitation (R&R) programme (also known as Cognitive Skills) which was first used by the Canadian Correctional System but has since been used more widely in a number of countries including the USA. Also increasingly popular is the use of the Enhanced Thinking Skills (ETS) programme. Courses involve teaching participants how to think more positively, to empathise with others, and to avoid situations and patterns of thinking and behaviour that have previously led to crime in the individual's past in order to avoid returning to crime. The use of such Offending Behaviour Programmes in the UK is on the increase, and around 6,000 prisoners completed an accredited offending behaviour programme in 2000/01 (SEU, 2002). By 2003/04 the Prison Service has a target of delivering 8,900 offending behaviour courses in prison and the Probation Service has a target of delivering 30,000 in the community. Described as 'one of the key building blocks in the programme of interventions to reduce reoffending' (Home Office, 2004b) prisoners in 108 establishments completed over 7,300 accredited programmes in 2002- 03 and over 8,900 in 2003-04. In 2002-03, over 7,700 Probation Service accredited programmes were completed, and this was almost doubled to over 13,100 in 2003-04 (ibid.).

Friendship et al (2003a) illustrate how the body of research initiated by Gendreau and Ross (1983) known as 'what works' research has led to the development of a 'strong treatment ethic' within the criminal justice system in the UK. This growing body of literature suggests that specific multi-modal cognitive-behavioural programmes are effective. Robinson and Porporino (2001) summarised many of the relevant 'what works' studies of offenders who completed the R&R programme between 1989 and 1994. They describe how one thinking skills intervention involving a sample of over 4,000 Canadian offenders resulted in a reduction in reconviction rates of 5 percentage points or 20.5%. According to Friendship et al., an evaluation in a British setting of a version of an R&R programme known as Straight Thinking on Probation (STOP) showed a seven percentage point or 35% reduction in reconviction, although this was not sustained in two and five year follow-up studies. The authors go on to describe how HM Prison Service in England and Wales started to run cognitive skills programmes in ten prison establishments in 1992, using an in-house version of R&R initially under the banner of Thinking Skills and latterly in 1993 as ETS. They point out that, while the Prison Service was aware of the 'what works' principles and had applied some of these into its programmes, this was done in a somewhat piecemeal way which was not always underpinned by a theoretical framework or empirical research supported by best practice. They acknowledge, however, that the accreditation system introduced in 1996 is beginning to address some of these issues.

A recent study reported that around 70 per cent of prisons run accredited offending behaviour programmes and that the number of prisoners completing programmes has grown significantly (NAO, 2002). However, the same study reported that there were significant regional differences in access to programmes, with numbers waiting to begin a particular course ranging from none in one prison to 450 in another. Waiting lists mean that prisoners who would have met the criteria are often released before they have had a chance to benefit from the programme. Despite their proven success (Falshaw et al., 2003; Cann et al., 2003), there is currently no reliable measure of the overall number of prisoners who would benefit from such Offending Behaviour Programmes. OBPs also vary in their intensity and cost, from £2,000 per prisoner for the Enhanced Thinking Skills course (around 40 hours) to around £7,000 per prisoner for programmes aimed at high security, violent prisoners (SEU 2002).

Most existing programmes are aimed at male adult prisoners serving sentences of over twelve months. Those serving short sentences are not usually in prison for long enough for the identification and assessment procedure to be completed, and often offenders are not in the same place long enough to obtain useful interventions (Carter, 2003). Selection for accredited courses is rigorous to ensure maximum success rates, but this can result in many of those with mental health problems or poor basic skills being unable to access accredited offending behaviour programmes, as it is felt that they will not be able to cope with the demands placed on them.

Movement of prisoners around the prison estate can also be problematic. The Prison Service has made significant efforts to ensure that those involved in accredited programmes are not subject to moves around the system, disrupting their attendance. However, there is no data on the numbers who are moved and recent work by the National Audit Office (2002) has found that only 34 per cent of prisons believed that those moved to their establishment would be able to continue with an offending behaviour programme. Additionally, specific groups may not fare as well: there are currently no accredited offending behaviour programmes designed *specifically* for women, young adult prisoners, or remand prisoners. One in two remand prisoners go on to receive a custodial sentence, and four out of five are found guilty (SEU, 2002). Yet they are unable to begin programmes designed to improve areas such as thinking skills during the remand period. The quality of interventions also varies greatly, and is dependent on the area in which the offender receives them (HM Inspectorate of Probation, 2002/3) and the National Audit Office concluded that: 'a prisoner's access to programmes still owes much to where they are sent' (NAO, 2002).

Education and Training Provision in England and Wales: Our Survey

So what is being offered in prisons today? A survey by the LSDA (Vorhaus, 2003) based on questionnaire returns from 91 prisons and Young Offender Institutions (YOIs) found that there was a considerable amount of 'spare capacity' in prison education and training provision, with only 5% of prisons and less than 1% of YOIs and Her Majesty's Prisons (HMP/YOIs) operating at, or near, full capacity. Overall, 38% of the prison population were engaged in full or part time education or training, the majority of these in part time education (21% of the total prison population). Young Offender Institutions were the most successful in terms of providing full and part time training places (12% and 10% of prisoners in YOIs) and full time education places (22% of prisoners in YOIs).

At the beginning of the present research, the team realised that there was no simple answer as to what was currently being offered in prisons and YOIs across England and Wales. There were many variables which shaped the provision of both education and training. For example, the different categories and types of prisons, whether they were private or

Institution	Full-time Ed	Part-time Ed	Full-time training	Part-time training	Total
HMP's	8%	23%	5%	<1%	36%
YOI's	22%	7%	12%	10%	51%
HMP/YOI	6%	23%	8%	3%	40%
Mean	9%	22%	6%	2%	38.6%

Adapted from Vorhaus, 2003: NB there may be an element of double-counting, with prisoners accessing both part and full time education and training.

state funded and if an institutions had a particular 'specialist' target population, all led to a huge variance in provision. It was working from this assumption that we felt we had a unique opportunity to gain an overall picture of education and training provision. More specifically, the team aimed to answer one particular research question: *How far do thinking skills approaches feature in the courses and training provided in HM Prisons?*

Although we wanted to explore the provision of thinking skills activities generally, we were also interested in what courses or activities prison staff actually perceived, and understood, to be either developing and/or extending prisoners' thinking skills. These could be educational courses, offender behaviour courses and vocational and non-vocational courses.

Responses

One-hundred and thirty-nine questionnaires were sent out to all prisons and young offender institutions in England and Wales, and 83 were returned. This gives an overall response rate of 60%. The team were aware that job titles and roles varied considerably across the prisons, and so questionnaires were sent directly to the governor (or director, in the case of private prisons) of each establishment, with a request that the survey was passed on to the most relevant person to complete.

Most completed questionnaires (56) from our sample were received from prisons, although this is not surprising given that prisons make up 72% (100) of all the institutions in England and Wales we surveyed. The response rate of 56% therefore was slightly lower than we anticipated. The response rate of HMP/YOI establishments was proportionately higher - 16 of a possible 24 - therefore representing a questionnaire response rate of 67%. Almost all YOI establishments responded (69%), and there was a 100% response rate from both Immigration Removal Centres (IRCs). However, it is worth noting here that both Immigration Removal Centres did not fully complete the questionnaire, as they reported that their work was not relevant to this survey.

Establishment Type	Questionnaire Count	% of sample	Establishment Count	% of all establishment
HMP	56	67	100	56
HMP/YOI	16	19	24	67
YOI	9	11	13	69
IRC	2	2	2	100
Total	83	100	139	

HMP – HM Prison; YOI – HM Young Offender Institution; IRC: Immigration Removal Centre.

The questionnaire return rate was initially very disappointing, and it often took several weeks for the questionnaire to arrive on the desk of the person most relevant to complete it; usually this being the Education Manager or Head of Learning and Skills.

The majority of questionnaires received (88%) were from establishments which detain only male prisoners. The response rate from female prisons was a little disappointing, with only 7 of the 17 (at the time of the survey) responding, which translates into an overall response rate of 41%.

Prisoner Gender	Questionnaire Count	% of sample	Establishment Count	% of all establishments
All Male	73	88	121	60
All Female	7	8	17	41
Not Specified	2	2	0	0
Both	1	1	1	100
Total	83	100	139	

The research also intended to explore how prison staff construe the idea of 'thinking skills' and therefore the questionnaire asked:

> Please identify up to eight courses offered in your institution, which **in your opinion** contain elements which **help to develop or extend prisoners' thinking skills.** These may be educational courses, offending behaviour courses, vocational or non-vocational courses.

Respondents were then asked:

> What is the emphasis on thinking skills in this course?
> (A) Its primary aim is to develop thinking;
> (B) The course aims to develop transferable skills; or
> (C) Thinking skills are required to deal with the course subject or activities.

Completed questionnaires were coded and data was entered and analysed using SPSS software, and selected results are presented here.

Course category	Count	% of sample
Educational	238	47
Psychological	202	39.5
Vocational	63	12
*Not categorised	6	1
**None	2	>0.5
Total	511	100

*Six courses were rated as A, B or C by respondents but could not be categorised as educational, vocational or psychological due to a lack of course information. **One institution did not provide any course information. Another provided course information, but did not provide course ratings.

Two establishments responded by saying that all courses promote thinking skills, but most nominated between one and ten courses (the median being six courses). Overall, 52% of the courses nominated were psychological in orientation, while 33% were educational and 15% vocational. For the 'A' rated courses alone (those where the primary aim is to develop thinking) the proportions were even more strongly weighted towards courses with a psychological orientation (77%), with 19% being educational courses and only 3% vocational.

It is clear that both educational and psychological courses are seen as aiming to develop effective thinking or as having a thinking skills emphasis. Vocational courses were mentioned less frequently, but this should not be taken to imply that thinking is less important in such courses. In fact, the ratio of vocational courses to educational courses mentioned (1: 3.8) is very similar to the ratio of prisoners attending such courses nationally (1: 3.6) (Vorhaus, 2003).

Course Category	Count	% of sample
A – where the primary aim is to develop thinking	161	32
B – which aim to develop transferable skills	247	48
C – where thinking skills are required	101	20
*None	2	0.4
Total	511	100

One establishment did not provide any course information. Another provided course information but did not provide course ratings.

The main finding of interest here is that about a third (31.5%) of all courses mentioned are thought to have the development of thinking as its primary aim. A further 48.3% of the courses are believed to develop transferable skills. If we assume that the thinking skills in the first group are thought of as transferable, this makes a total 80% of the courses mentioned which are thought to equip prisoners with transferable skills.

A summary below (*Table 6*) illustrates how different types of nominated course were rated (excluding courses which were mentioned only once). It can be seen that the psychological 'What Works' courses are seen as being primarily about thinking (as their titles suggest). Educational courses in literacy, numeracy and Key Skills Communication (discussion, reading and writing) are sometimes also seen in these terms, but more often as aiming to develop transferable skills. Vocational courses tend to get lower ratings.

Name or type of course	n	Comments
Enhanced Thinking Skills	17	These were all 'A' rated.
Reasoning and Rehabilitation	7	
Motivating Offenders to Rethink Everything	3	
Social and life skills	30	16 were 'A' rated
Drugs and/or alcohol abuse courses	13	9 were 'A' rated
Key Skills Problem Solving	2	
Anger management	7	3 were 'A' rated
Literacy/numeracy	21	8 'A' ratings 12 'B' ratings
Key skills communications	9	3 'A' ratings 5 'B' ratings
Art	2	
Brickwork	3	
IT/computing	15	10 'B' ratings 4 'C' ratings

What stands out most from this analysis is that respondents (who were generally education personnel) clearly saw the family of cognitive skill programmes (often known as thinking skills programmes) as having the primary aim of developing thinking. ETS and R&R featured very strongly here. However, it is also worth noting that courses dealing with drugs and alcohol abuse were also predominantly A-rated, as were a variety of psychology-based courses such as Anger Management.

Of the education courses mentioned there were five types which received the same number or more A-ratings in comparison with B or C ratings:

- General education courses;
- Citizenship;
- Personal development;
- Key Skills, problem-solving; and
- Health-related courses.

Other types of course where a significant minority gave A-ratings were: Literacy and Numeracy and Key Skills Communication.

The vast majority of education courses, including Key Skills (such as Information Technology, team-working and communication skills), literacy and numeracy, business studies, sports-related, food-related and arts-related courses were seen as primarily seeking to develop transferable skills rather than to develop thinking as such. This was also true of courses dealing with group work and resettlement. Of the twenty courses dealing with Social and Life Skills, 5 were A-rated, with 10 receiving B ratings and 10 being C-rated. The only type of course where the highest number of C ratings were given was Basic Skills. These last two findings may give cause for concern, as it suggests that the terminology itself may affect perceptions – or else that basic skills and social skills are seen as a low-level set of subskills (e.g. phonic skills, multiplication skills or greeting skills). No work-related courses were given A-ratings, but there were 34 B-ratings and 12 C-ratings. This brings out the perceived importance of transferable skills in such courses.

In the questionnaire respondents were asked to list vocational and non-vocational courses offered in their establishments, apart from any nominated courses. They were also asked to specify the size of groups for all nominated and non-nominated courses, to see if courses rated high for 'thinking skills' tended to have smaller groups. We found that this was not the case, as all types of course had an average of 9 or 10 participants. Whether this figure represents those enrolled rather than those actually present in a typical session is not known. Nor is it known how this figure has come to be the norm in prison education and training. However, with groups of nine or ten it is certainly possible for dialogue and discussion to take place as well as for individuals and subgroups to work at tasks and then have time to present, or report back.

Conclusions

Overall it was interesting that significant numbers of staff in prisons are aware of the importance of thinking skills in the education and training provided in prisons. The notion of transferable skills is also salient for many. What is less clear is whether courses are delivered in such a way that course participants are able to make connections between them, thereby increasing the possibility that they will be able to generalise their knowledge and skills both within and outside the prison setting. Certainly within prisons there have been arguments that education generally should be more closely integrated with programmes on social skills, substance abuse, anger management and family violence (Townsend, 1991). Newman *et al* wrote about the 'right kind' of education in United States correctional facilities, and took it to include:

- moral education
- democratic self-rule in the 'just community'
- instruction in the humanities, with a strong appeal to the cognitive
- training in a variety of skills to enable the prisoner to cope with the personal, sexual, familial, chemical, economic, vocational, and social problems of life, thereby to gain a realistic sense of one's individual worth as a human being (Newman *et al.*, 1993).

Learning and generalisation is difficult in stressful environments. Prisons are arguably prime examples of such environments, and some research has documented that prisoners see their environment as a place of danger which generates and shapes conflict (Edgar and Martin, 2002). Such stressful environments will then, inevitably, impact on learning, and particularly on transfer and generalisation. So if we are going to try and teach generalisation and transferability, what would be the most profitable area to choose? Oral communication could be regarded as being the most profitable as skills learnt could be used by prisoners for the remainder of their lives, both inside and outside of prison.

Friendship *et al* (2003b), while accepting that reconviction rates are a fundamental measure of success or failure, claim that they cannot be considered in isolation from other empirically related treatment and resettlement factors. They offer an integrated model for the evaluation of accredited cognitive behaviour interventions which includes pre- and post-treatment psychometric tests, participants' own feedback on the benefit of treatment, treatment summary documents and daily assessments from prison staff such as wing logs and adjudication records, together with the assessments made by group facilitators. They say that changes in intermediary treatment targets, for instance socialisation and impulsivity, are best monitored on a day-to-day basis when the skills acquired during therapy are put to the test. The same authors believe that the following factors are key to the effectiveness of any cognitive intervention and should therefore be part of the criteria for evaluation studies:

- group climate, characterised by high cohesion, good organisation and being well led by facilitators

- encouragement of the open expression of feelings
- a sense of group responsibility
- a sense of hope among group members, coupled with an institutional climate where prison staff are involved in treatment and model appropriate attitudes and behaviour.

Thinking skills in schools are presented as embedded in curriculum or separately delivered. There is some evidence to suggest that these generic, cognitive thinking skills are more easily assimilated by students when part of mathematics, science and literacy lessons (Higgins et al. 2004), and that there is more evidence that these skills are transferable (e.g. Adey and Shayer, 1990). Even if, as the survey suggests, there are elements of thinking skills in a good deal of current provision, there has been, and continues to be, an increased use in the UK for stand-alone thinking skills programmes like ETS and R&R. Home Office projections and current forecasts estimate that by 2009 there will be 93,000 offenders in custody and 300,000 under supervision in the community (Carter 2003). It seems that Offending Behaviour Programmes such as ETS and R&R will continue to play a major role in the rehabilitation and education of offenders both within prison and in the community.

Bibliography

Adey, P. and Shayer, M. (1990); Accelerating the development of formal thinking in middle and high school students. *Journal of Research in Science Teaching* 27(3): pp 267-285.

Cann, J., Falshaw, L., Nugent, F. and Friendship, C. (2003); Understanding What Works: accredited cognitive skills programmes for adult men and young offenders. Home Office Online Findings No. 226 on http://www.homeoffice.gov.uk/rds/pdfs2/r226.pdf [accessed 27/01/05].

Carter, P. (2003); Managing Offenders, Reducing Crime: A new approach. London: Strategy Unit.

Criminal Justice Act (2003); Chapter 44, London: HMSO.

Edgar, K. and Martin, C. (2002); Conflicts and Violence in Prison. ESRC Violence Research Programme, Summary Findings on http://www1.rhbnc.ac.uk/sociopolitical-science/vrp/Findings/rfedgar.PDF [accessed 27/01/05].

Falshaw, L., Friendship, C., Travers, R and Nugent, F. (2003); Searching for 'What Works': an evaluation of cognitive skills programmes. Home Office Online Findings No. 206 on www.homeoffice.gov.uk/rds/pdfs2/r206.pdf [accessed 27/01/05].

Friendship, C., Blud, L. Erikson, M. Travers, R. and Thornton, D. (2003a); Cognitive behavioural treatment for imprisoned offenders: An evaluation of HM Prison Service's cognitive skills programmes. *Legal and Criminological Psychology*, 8, 103-114.

Friendship, C., Falshaw, L. and Beech, A. R. (2003b); Measuring the real impact of accredited offending behaviour programmes. *Legal and Criminological Psychology*, 8, 115-127.

Gendreau, P. & Ross, R.R. (1983) Success in corrections: Programs and principles. In R. R. Corrado (ed.), Juvenile Justice. Toronto, OT: Butterworths.

Hall, I, Hardman, F, Smith, F. and Taverner, S. (1999); The Relevance of GCSE Mathematics and English as Preparation for Employment. *Journal of Vocational Education and Training*, 51(2), 283-305.

Higgins, S., Baumfield, V., Lin, M., Moseley, D., Butterworth, M., Downey, G., Gregson, M., Rockett, M., Oberski, I. and Thacker, D. (2004); Thinking skills approaches to effective teaching and learning: what is the evidence for impact on learners? London: The EPPI-Centre, Institute of Education.

HM Inspectorates of Prisons and Probation (2001); Through the Prison Gate: a Joint Thematic Review. London, Home Office.

HM Inspectorate of Probation (2002/03); Annual Report. London: HM Inspectorate of Probation.

HM Prison Service (2001); Annual Report and Accounts. London: HM Prison Service.

HM Prison Service (2003); Annual Report: Improving Prisoners' Prospects on Release. London: HM Prison Service.

Hogarth, T., Wilson, R.A, Shury, J., Vivian, D. and Winterbotham, M. (2004); National Employers Skills Survey 2003: Key Findings. Coventry: Learning and Skills Council.

Home Office (2004a); Reducing Crime - Changing Lives. London: Home Office.

Home Office (2004b); Reducing Re-offending: National Action Plan. London: Home Office.

Home Office (2004c); Reducing Re-offending: National Action Plan - A Reference Document. London: Home Office.

Moseley, D.V., Baumfield, V., Higgins, S., Mei Lin, Miller, J., Newton, D., Robson, S., Elliott, J. and Gregson, M. (2004); Thinking skill frameworks for post-16 learners: an evaluation. London: Learning and Skills Research Centre.

National Audit Office (2002); Reducing Prisoner Reoffending. London: National Audit Office.

Newman, A.P.; Lewis, W.; and Beverstock, C. (1993); Prison Literacy: Implications for Program and Assessment Policy. National Centre on Adult Literacy Technical Report. TR93-1 September 1993, co-published with ERIC Clearinghouse on Reading and Communication Skills, Bloomington Indiana.

Pawson, R. (2000); The Evaluator's Tale. In D. Wilson and A. Reuss, (Eds.) Prison(er) Education: stories of change and transformation. Winchester: Waterside Press.

Robinson, D. and Porporino, F.J. (2001); Programming in cognitive skills: the Reasoning and Rehabilitation Program. In C. Hollin (ed.); Handbook of Offender Assessment and Treatment. Chichester: Wiley.

Social Exclusion Unit (2002); Reducing Reoffending by Ex-Prisoners. London: Social Exclusion Unit.

Townsend, T. (1991); Foreword. Forum on Corrections Research, 3(1), 2. Correctional Service Canada.

Vorhaus, J. (2003); Education, Training, Assessment and Learner Support in HM Prisons and Young Offender Institutions, A Preliminary Study. London: Learning and Skills Development Agency.

Wilson, D.H., Gallagher, C.A. and MacKenzie, D.L. (2000); A meta-analysis of corrections-based education, vocation and work-based programs for adult offenders. Journal of Research in Crime and Delinquency, 37(4), 347-368.

Worrall, J. (2004); The impact of education on young men in prison. Journal of Offender Education, 1(May): 1-21.

The Road to Rehabilitation: A Personal Journey through Prison Education

Noel 'Razor' Smith

I have spent almost three decades in and out of prison and laboured under many educational regimes. I entered the prison system as an illiterate child, and i was not alone; according to Home Office figures 130,000 people are or have been in prison in this country in any one year and 81% of these have educational skills that are below level 1. Finally, in the 21st century, the prison system is waking up to the concept that without education you can not have rehabilitation. The system has become proactive in giving prisoners at least a basic level of education but, though this is better than no education at all, it is not good enough. Like most attempts at rehabilitating prisoners in this country, educating only to basic skills level is a half-hearted effort. People with poor educational skills will always be attracted to crime and the financial rewards it offers, you don't have to have a GCSE to throw a brick through a jewellers window or cosh a security guard and there are no interviews for these jobs. I committed my own crimes not because I was evil and enjoyed hurting people, but because there were few other opportunities for me to get the status and money that I craved in the straight world. The reason that our reconviction rates are so high is because we learn nothing in prison and are released back into the same position that caused us to take up crime in the first place. Prison is all wasted time and opportunity for most prisoners, a mere conveyor belt that takes us from dead-end to dead-end. It is shameful that a man can spend a decade or more in prison and come out without any sort of skill or educational qualification that would be of use in the outside world, and yet this is what is happening. Criminals are, on the whole, reckless with other people's property and lives because they have no self-worth themselves, and here I speak from experience. Being given the encouragement and opportunity to gain useful educational qualifications whilst in prison could be a way of lowering the reconviction rates and, in my humble, but qualified, opinion it is about time we gave it a try. If anyone is really serious about lowering crime rates and rehabilitating criminals then surely education is the key? As an example of how this might work I offer my own experiences with prison and education.

As a child growing up in London I somehow managed to avoid everything but the most basic of education. My family were forever moving from one dingy hovel to another and that meant I didn't get a chance to settle for long in any one school. I picked up a bit of spelling here, a bit of reading there and I knew enough to write my own name and that was all I needed as far as I was concerned. School was too dull for me, I preferred the excitement of the streets.

By the time my family had settled down in a council flat in Lambeth and I was sent to Tulse Hill Secondary Modern school I was already an educational lost cause. I attended Tulse Hill for approximately 3 three months, during which time I learned absolutely nothing as I spent most of my day fighting a selection of the 1200 other inner-city youth that made up the school's intake. For the next 3 years I played truant and nobody even noticed.

At the age of 14, I was arrested for the theft of a motorcycle and sentenced to three months detention at Her Majesty's Detention Centre Send, in Woking. These were days of the 'Short Sharp Shock', when those in charge of the penal policy thought that the way to a young lawbreaker's conscience was through his arse with a size ten boot, in much the same way as sixteenth century peasants believed they could drive the devil out of lonely old women by burning them at the stake. Along with the standard thumping on reception at HMDC Send I was given an education test. I can only assume that I failed the test, but even though I was still two years under the school leaving age I was put to work digging up fields.

In 2002 I applied for my prison records under the auspices of The Data Protection Act 1998 and was interested to find that some of my reports dated back to my juvenile days. One, from HMDC Send, says that I was of 'well below average intelligence, bordering on educationally (sic) subnormal'. Another states – 'Smith has been identified as one of a group of boys who will spend the rest of his life in and out of institutions'. For 'security reasons' the names of the report writers have been blanked out on my copies. So, at the age of 14, I was already categorised, pigeonholed and judged fit only for manual labour.

When I left HMDC Send, having served my sentence, I found that Tulse Hill school did not want me back. I was offered a place at Henry Thornton secondary school, but when I failed to turn up in he appointed day no search parties were sent looking for me and that was the end of my sporadic schooling. Had I been able to read I might have seen the writing on the wall, but I went straight back into crime and it was not long before I once again found myself in the dock.

In May 1977, at the age of 16, I stood in the dock of the Old Bailey being sentence to 3 years detention under Section 53 of The Children and Young Persons Act 1933. The definition of the Section 53 sentence is that it should be given to 'any young person, under the age of 18, who has committed a crime that would warrant a sentence of 14 years or more for an adult'. I had been charged with armed robbery, possession of firearms and grievous bodily harm. I had been on remand since the previous February at Latchmere House juvenile remand centre in Surrey and, though I was still an 'USLA' (jargon for juveniles who are Under School Leaving Age), I had caused enough trouble so the authorities would allow me to be housed with the 'young adult prisoners' rather than with the USLAs. This meant that education was not compulsory for me.

My first stop as a Section 53 detained was a special unit for violent juveniles at Ashford remand centre in Middlesex. Classes here were compulsory but even if they weren't I would have volunteered just to get out of my cell for a couple of hours a day. Education for us seemed to consist of plenty of arts and crafts. On Monday afternoons we drew and painted, on Tuesday and Thursday we stuffed and sewed soft toys and on Wednesday and Friday we made pottery. We were particularly loud and violent group of kids in that unit and I suppose that these classes were designed to keep us quiet. And despite the fact that none of us were exactly overflowing with even the basics of education, no attempt was made to really educate us in anything but arts and crafts.

My next step in the juvenile process saw me allocated to Dover borstal. At Dover I was given the same reception education test I had received at HMDC Send three years before. I have no idea whether I was due to receive any education at Dover because I became very a difficult detainee at this stage and spent the bulk of my time here in solitary confinement in the punishment block before being ghosted to the hospital wing at Rochester borstal for 'mental observation'.

In the hospital wing at Rochester is wall all forced medication and padded cells, though I did get the seemingly obligatory soft-toy making 'class' twice a week for as long as I was there. Once I had been deemed sane I was put back on a wing on normal location within Rochester, but this didn't last due to me assaulting a prison officer whilst attempting to escape. It was during the long months I spent in solitary confinement for these charges that I made my first real step toward getting myself educated. The punishment block at Rochester was minimalism taken to its extremes. My whole world consisted of a six-by-four foot cell with one barred window that was covered on the inside by a sheet of opaque perspex, a plastic chamber pot, a plank bench and table screwed into the wall and a wafer-thin mattress that was removed every morning at 7am and returned at 8pm. I spent 24 hours of every day in this cell except for half an hour on Saturday afternoons when I was allowed to walk twenty paces along the landing to have a shower. My world, at the age of 17, was a very small one.

The great enemy in solitary confinement is boredom and for the first 6 weeks I passed the long days and night by exercising, singing, whistling and going over in my memory every film I had ever seen. There was rule of silence in the punishment block so the singing and whistling had to be kept to a whisper and an intake of breath. One thing that I was allowed to have in the cell and which would certainly have gone far to relieve the boredom was a book. Unfortunately for, I couldn't read. Then, one day, I had a visit from a catholic priest. I had given my religion as catholic when I had entered prison merely because I had grown up as one, but in reality I had no interest in religion whatsoever. I was glad to see this priest though and it was a treat to be able to talk out loud to someone who wasn't a screw. The priest asked me what I did with my days and, when I told him, he asked me why I didn't avail myself of the small library in the block and I had to admit my educational shortcomings.

The next day the priest was back and had brought me a thin book which I recall was about a dog called spot and the plot was to draw attention to his running abilities. E sat on the floor of my cell and went through the book with me a couple of times. Maybe I had absorbed, by osmosis I suspect, more from the few school classes I had attended than I had thought, or maybe I was driven by the sheer terror I was starting to feel when it came to boredom but I seemed to pick up on reading very quickly. After two weeks I was able to hold my own with such classics as 'The Three Pirates' and 'Red Indians'.

I know it is a bit of a cliché, but being able to read opened a whole new world for me. I never tired of the novelty of being able to look at letters and words on a page and make sense of them. I became hungry for reading, I would read anything and everything and every time I picked up a book I had not yet read I would be literally shaking with the excitement of anticipation. Books banished the boredom of solitary confinement and allowed me to escape the confines of my cold and barren cell. The rest of my time in solitary seemed to pass quickly now that I could fill the days with reading. Eventually I was released from solitary and allowed back up onto the wing but I took my reading addiction with me and fed it daily. Because of my, by now, atrocious record of violence and non co-operation I was deemed too unstable to be put on classes, most of which were run by civilians, and I was instead allocated a place on a vocational training course. The borstal system was big on vocational training and Rochester had VTCs for plumbing, bricklaying, motor-mechanics, draughtsmen, painting and decorating and something called 'Skilled Ops', which basically taught a bit of everything about the building trade. If given a choice I would have chosen motor-mechanics, draughtsmen or plumbing to train in, but my education test ruled me out for these occupations because they involved reading and maths. Though I had now learned to read my test results, taken on entry to prison, said otherwise and were never updated. So I ended up on Skilled Ops and became a glorified builder's labourer.

Though I had now learned to read I still had no desire to take my education further. I was getting all the education I needed from reading books and being entertained at the same time. I got into the habit, which persists to this day, of having three different books on the go at the same time. So I might read a couple of chapters of a biography and then pick up an adventure story and read a few chapters before turning to a history book. It meant I was never bored and I was also learning as I read. By day I filled concrete moulds for paving slabs and by night I read until lights out at 10pm, and this is how I served out the rest of my sentence.

Released in May 1980, having served every last day of my Section 53 sentence, I went back to crime very quickly. I was 19 years old, with not a single educational qualification to my name and no work record. But at least, If I had been so inclined, I could have read the vacancy cards in the job centre. I just wasn't inclined to.

Over the next decade I was in and out of prison and learned absolutely nothing that would be of any use outside of the criminal world. I can now see that learning to read had been a bit of a mixed blessing for me in that it made prison bearable. I would literally read away my short sentences and periods on remand, devouring a book a day most days. Prison held no fear for me, boredom being my only real enemy, and books had that covered.

By 1990 I was a couple of years into a 19 year sentence for armed robbery at HMP Wandsworth. I was 29 years old and with the bleak vista of another decade in prison facing me I got the idea that now might be a good time to do a few classes. There were no full time education classes for long-term prisoners at Wandsworth but we were allowed to apply for two evening classes per week. I put down for music and art. I learned to play the tenor saxophone and painted pictures of dark and gloomy landscapes for a couple of months. I was while I was attending evening classes in the education department that I saw a poster asking if anyone wanted to do an Open University course.

The idea of actually getting a degree began to intrigue me. It wasn't as if I was short of the time to do it in, four years was like a drop in the ocean with my sentence, and I had now read enough to not seriously embarrass myself in most subjects. I decided to apply and see what happened. This was the first time that HMP Wandsworth had ever funded prisoners for the Open University and they only had eight places on offer so there was to be a selection process. Eleven prisoners from D wing, the long term wing, applied for the course and were all told to write a book review to a maximum of 300 words. I chose the book I was actually reading as that moment, which was John Steinbeck's 'Cannery Row', and carefully set about crafting my review. I was very pleased with the finished review as it was the first serious writing I had ever done and I thought I definitely had a good chance of getting one of the available places on the course. I submitted my work to the education department and began the long wait to see if I had been accepted.

In the meantime I went about serving my prison sentence in much the way I always had, by getting involved in as much trouble as I could. I got involved in an attempted escape that went fairly wrong fairly quickly and ended up in a pitched battle between prisoners and screws that finished in a bit of a bloodbath. Instead of crashing out of HMP Wandsworth on the back of a hijacked JCB digger I found myself once more facing months of solitary confinement in the punishment block. I was charged with assaulting prison staff and attempting to incite a riot and this was to have a knock-on effect on my application for the Open University. I was told by a tutor from the education department that I was not one of the eight who had been chosen.

Officially it was because my book review was not good enough, but, perhaps of conscience, she told me 'unofficially' that it was because I had assaulted prison officers and they had the last word. I just had to accept it. But at least I could take comfort in the thought that my book review had not been that bad.

In 1991, whilst at HMP Albany on the Isle of Wight, I began to write poetry and came second in a Christmas poetry competition held by the education department. Encouraged by this I became partners with another prisoner in a black market customised greeting card making business. I supplied the verse and my partner, a Grenadian drug smuggler, supplied the artwork. We sold our cards to our fellow prisoners and did roaring trade. This was the first time I realised that there might be profit in being able to write. It was around this time that I saw an advert in Inside-time, the only national prison newspaper, from a Probation Officer in Sheffield, called Julian Broadhead, who was starting a journal of prisoner's writing. The journal was to be called, appropriately enough, Prison Writing, and would feature poetry and prose from prisoners here and abroad. But the part that really interested me was that he was offering a 'small payment' for any work he used in the journal. I decided to have a crack at writing something.

I submitted two poems and an account of the attempted escape from HMP Wandsworth to Prison Writing and, in truth, I expected to hear no more. Scribbling rhyming couplets for prison-made greeting cards was one thing, but, with my lack of formal education and no real writing experience, I thought I was probably out of my league. At that time there were around 48,000 prisoners in this country alone and I was sure that plenty of them would be tempted to write some just as I had. But, as we say in prison (where all forms of gambling are banned) – you can't win the lottery if you don't buy a ticket.

About a month after my submissions I received a letter from Julian Broadhead saying that he had accepted all three of my pieces for the journal and asking me if I had written anything else that he might be able to use for future editions. His letter was full of praise for my writing style, which was a shock to me as I didn't even know I had a writing style! I can still recall how proud and excited I was to read and reread this letter. I could hardly believe it that anyone outside would want to read what I had to write, let alone publish it in an international journal and pay me for it. It was this letter that inspired me to take writing seriously and to seek some formal education. I had never been praised for anything before in my life, except by other criminals for pulling off a daring blag or sticking a right-hander on a screw, that sort of thing, so this was the first stop on my road to Damascus.

Unfortunately one hymn doesn't make saint and writing and education had to take a back seat for a few months as I escaped from prison and went on a bit of a rampage. But when I was re-arrested and back in custody there was a nice surprise waiting for me. Whilst I had been unlawfully at large the edition of Prison Writing which featured my poetry and prose had been released to much critical acclaim and one of my poems, 'Old Lags', had been selected as a Poem of the Day by The Independent newspaper. It was such a buzz to see something that I had written appearing in a national daily broadsheet that not even the prospect of another fifteen years added to my prison sentence could take the shine off it. Soon afterwards I received a request from BBC Radio 4 to interview me about my poetry for an edition of a programme called Stanza, which was about prison poetry. I accepted and it was great to hear my poetry broadcast on national radio. I began to think that I might have stumbled upon a talent that could possibly change my life in some way and decided that it was time to take my writing seriously and apply for some long overdue education.

One of the things that was to frustrate me about prison education was the fact that any prisoner who applied to go onto full time education had to be prepared to suffer a financial penalty. The average weekly wage for education is around £7, compared to £30 plus for the prisoner who chooses to work in the prison workshops. It is the same in every prison I have been in and this financial disparity creates a dilemma for a lot of prisoners. Prison workshops are full of prisoners putting nuts into bolts or folding plastic bags who could be learning to read and write or even furthering whatever education they already have, unfortunately there is very little incentive for them. I can only speculate on the reason for the prison authorities making education a very poor prospect compared to workshops but I believe it is to do with money. Most of the mind-numbing labour done in prison workshops is for commercial companies who make a good profit on the back of prison workers and no doubt spread a bit of that profit in the direction of the prisons themselves. And, in my opinion, if prisoners could earn as much by taking education classes then a lot more would chose that option. Some people may wonder why a prisoner would need money inside a prison? After all, it's not as if we have to pay rent or other bills? In fact, serving a prison sentence can be a pretty expensive business.

Since 1991 prisoners have been allowed access to pay phones in order to keep in touch with family and friends in the outside world, and also to access solicitors and other legal bodies. Every prison in this country has at least one such phone on every wing and this is a good thing, but they are very expensive to use. Unlike people outside, prisoners have no opportunity to shop around for the best deal when it comes to any of their purchases and this includes phone charges. Prison phones are charged at the same rate as the peak time public pay phones on the outside, there is no reduction in charges for phoning after 6 o clock or at weekends and it works out at around 10p per minute. Great profits for BT, but not so good for someone whose weekly wage is £7.

Prison canteens are, on the whole, also run by private companies who are in it to make a profit and, as we can hardly shop elsewhere, their prices reflect their monopoly status. Also most prisons now operate a policy whereby anything allowed in possession by prisoners must be purchased via a recognised catalogue system, including clothing. To give you an example of how expensive this can be – if I wish to purchase a pair of socks I can only get them in a pack of 3 pairs from the catalogue. The socks themnselves will cost £4.95 and the postage and packing will add another £3.50 to my outlay plus 30p for the outgoing stamp making a total of £8.75 for a pair of socks what my wife would probably pick up in a market and send for less than a pound. So that is why most prisoners choose prison workshops over prison education.

With my new-found success in the writing world I made up my mind to do something about my education. By the time I was in a brand new prison, HMP Highdown, which had a governor who was progressive enough to realise that education is an aid to rehabilitation. Governor Stephen Pryor was all for getting prisoners out of their cells and into education and useful activities, he set up a computer workshop with state of the art equipment, a well equipped education department and a printing course. The one thing he had no control over was the wage levels for education as these are set by national policy, but he did allow prisoners to turn up at the education department and computer workshops to get a flavour of what was going on before they made up their minds. This was unheard of in other prisons. The head of education, Eileen Jackman, was also very proactive in pushing the value of educational classes and when I approached her about taking on an A-level correspondence class in law she was willing to back me via funding for the course despite my poor educational record and the fact that I had never done a single exam.

The early years of the 1990s were really the golden age of prison education in this country. It was an all too brief honeymoon period between the Woolf Report, into the causes of the Strangeways riots, which recommended a complete overhaul of our still Victorian prison system with more emphasis to be put on education and rehabilitation for prisoners, and the arrival of Michael Howard, in my opinion, the most reactionary and punishment-hungry Home Secretary ever. By May 1993 I had successfully completed my first A-level and received funding from HMP Highdown's education department to take a correspondence course on freelance feature writing with the London School of Journalism. Governor Pryor had heard the broadcast of my work on Radio 4 and asked me if I would be interested in starting a magazine for prisoners. I was given access to computers, printing press and a small budget and told to see what I could do.

'Sorted', the in-house magazine of HMP Highdown, ran for 18 months and 10 issues, picking up a Koestler Award for best new magazine along the way. The editorial team consisted of three prisoners, including myself, and an English teacher from the education department with Eileen Jackman in overall charge and Governor Pryor as the only censor.

Producing *Sorted* was a great education for me and I learned by trial and error. In conjunction with my work as writer and editor on *Sorted*, I completed my course with the LSJ and received an Honours diploma, one of only two handed out that year. I was now in my 30s, with a long prison sentence in front of me, and hungry for more educational achievement. I decided to try to get funding to try for a degree in criminology, a subject that I was starting to take an interest in, but once more I was to be defeated by a change in circumstances.

All too soon Michael Howard took over the rains of the Home Office and turned his gaze on the prison system. Prison education budgets were cut to the bone and emphasis was put on work for prisoners rather than education. In a very short time the computer and printing workshop at HMP Highdown was shut down, as was the charity workshop where prisoners were learning to repair wheelchairs for a local hospital charity. The plans for a motor mechanics course were scrapped, and *Sorted*, the award winning prison magazine, had its small budget taken away and had to fold. I was informed that HMP Highdown could no longer afford to fund anyone for correspondence courses or degrees. Soon both Governor Pryor and Eileen Jackman had moved on to other jobs and I was transferred back to HMP Albany, on the Isle of Wight, to be allocated a job in a workshop, making prison lockers.

For the next four years prison education was a bit of a bleak and barren landscape. It was like going back to the 1970s. I could do evening classes in soft-toy making or art, but if I wanted to do anything more mentally stimulating I would have to fund it myself. At this time I had no idea that there were charities such as the Prisoners' Education Trust who were willing to fund prisoners for further education courses. Allowing prisoners access to even the most basic of information was not big under Howard's reign. I bought myself a portable typewriter after coming 2nd in a short-story competition and spent a lot of my time honing my writing skills as best I could. I managed to get the odd piece published, including a couple of articles for *The Guardian*, and got a regular slot in a magazine for the legal profession called *The New Law Journal*. I kept on contributing written articles, poetry and short stories to *Prison Writing* and *Inside-Time*, but my dream of doing a degree in criminology stayed just that, a dream.

I was released in August 1997, went straight back to robbing banks for a living, and by August 1998 I was back in prison looking at a life sentence under the two-strikes law. Whilst on remand in HMP Belmarsh I was pleasantly surprised to find a decent education department in this prison. I was accepted onto a computer course and managed to achieve levels 1 and 2 in Computer Literacy and Information Technology (CLAIT). I was also inspired to write once more and contributed bits and pieces to various prison-based magazines and newspapers but my big journalistic break came when ex-cabinet minister Jonathan Aitken, jailed for perjury, was housed two cells away from mine. There was a media frenzy going on over Aitken, made more frenzied by the fact that no journalist could reach him in the top-security confines of HMP Belmarsh. Armed with the knowledge and experience I had gained from my course with the LSJ I approached Aitken and asked him if he would be willing to give me an exclusive interview. I must have been pretty persuasive because even after all the trouble he's had with journalists he agreed.

My two interviews with Jonathan Aitken were published by *Punch* magazine and picked up by the national press. On the back of this I was offered a regular slot in Punch as their prisons correspondent. After being sentenced to life imprisonment I was transferred to HMP Whitemoor, where, due to my CLAIT certificates and LSJ diploma, I was offered a job as subeditor on the Whitemoor magazine, W.I.S.E, and continued writing for outside newspapers and magazines. I made enquiries about the possibility of working for a degree course, but the prison system also frowned on any serving prisoner who wished to study criminology! I was astounded at this and asked the reasons behind it. I was told that recently a high profile prisoner had gained a degree in criminology at another prison and when they let him out on parole to pick up his reward he did not return. Instead he went on a bank robbing spree. So now the unofficial line on criminology studies was that they were to be discouraged. I know how incredible this must sound to anyone with no experience of prison Security Departments, but logic had never been their forte. So I decided to put my attempt at degree on hold.

I had met the author Will Self during my brief period of freedom in 1997 and found that he liked my short-stories, so I sent him my latest from Whitemoor and we began to correspond. Eventually Will began to visit me and encouraged me to write my life story with a view to publication. Will offered to act as my agent and I began my most ambitious writing project ever. I had written short-stories of up to 5000 words but I surprised even myself when I finished my manuscript with a word count of 211,000 words.

'A Few Kind Words and A Loaded Gun – the autobiography of a career criminal' was accepted for publication by Penguin and released in hardback to a flurry of good reviews. The book began to sell all over the world and the feedback was, on the whole, very positive. The most negative reaction was from the prison system who, after an initial interview with The Guardian, refused me permission to do press interviews about the book. By now I had volunteered for the therapeutic regime of HMP Grendon, a category B prison, near Aylesbury, which as the lowest reconviction rate for long-term violent offenders in the system. The success of my autobiography reawakened an urge for further education and HMP Grendon was willing and able to help me with this.

At Grendon I was encouraged to join the National Union of Journalists course which is run in the education department of the prison. The course, which is in four modules, covers every aspect of journalism and provides practical experience as it is combined with the production of 'Feedback', the Grendon magazine. Though the NUJ course is pretty comprehensive I also decided to try a correspondence course as well just to get another angle on it. I found a freelance journalism course that was available from ICS and applied for funding. I was informed by the education department at Grendon that they could not afford to fund correspondence courses, but this time I was pointed in the direction of the Prisoners' Education Trust, a charity that was prepared to fund courses for prisoners.

I completed my journalism course with ICS with and average score of 96% in all sections. I also completed level one of the NUJ course with a distinction and I am awaiting the results of my exams level two. I intend to complete modules three and four in the next two years. Not too shabby for a kid who entered prison thirty years ago unable to read and write. It has been a long and winding road for me and I have seen many changes to the prison education system. I am now 44 years old and facing the possibility of another half decade behind bars. The good news is that for the first time in my life I really feel as though I have the tools and understanding to have a future free of crime and imprisonment. Though I may be imprisoned for the next few years education had given me the means to compete in the outside world, a chance I've never had before, and I look forward to it.

When it came to getting educated in prison I was fairly lucky in the end, though I did stumble around for three decades. Had I not received encouragement from people outside of prison due to my writing reaching a wider audience I might be sitting here none the wiser and with only more imprisonment on the horizon. I have met men who, after 20 years of imprisonment, still cannot read and write, and this cannot be right. I still harbour a dream that I might take that elusive degree in criminology one day, but in today's prison system it will remain a dream. Since the realisation by Government that offending behaviour can be linked to lack of education most prison departments are now interested only in targeting for Basic Skills and little else. It is like putting a sticking plaster over a gaping wound, but quotas have got to be filled and boxes ticked in our Key Performance Indicator linked prison system. Despite the changes to the system, education is still too much of a low priority in our prisons. Compared to the drone-work of prison workshops prison education remains a poorly paid and unattractive prospect to the average prisoner. And until this financial disparity is rectified it will remain so.

The way in which the prison system has handicapped education in favour of workshops is almost criminal and if, as I do, you believe that education is the route to rehabilitation, then you must question the purpose of prison.

Sentenced to a Term of Education: Teacher Education Programmes in Prisons

Phil Bayliss

Introduction

The voices of teachers, managers and participants in education programmes specifically for those who teach in prison are heard in this chapter. The partnership between a university, an education contractor and prisons was formed to attract new teachers into the prison sector and later to qualify practising teachers. Now, more than 150 new and existing prison teachers, including uniformed instructors, vocational trainers and prisoner-orderlies, have gained a national teaching qualification, a Post-Graduate Certificate in Education (PGCE) or Certificate in Education (Cert Ed). As a progression from this qualification and as part of staff development, about ninety professional prisoner educators will have completed a specialist Master's module in Offender Education by 2006.

The nature and the aims of these programmes are critically evaluated. The rewards and obstacles of teaching those new to the profession and those with experience, including mixed groups of prisoners and staff in prison, are analysed. Pseudonyms are used for all prisons.

Background to the Programme

> ...in our prisons there are more people being taught basic literacy and numeracy, more being treated and detoxified for substance use problems, more being offered mental health support than in any other public institution. (Owers, 2005)

As HM Chief Inspector of Prisons, Anne Owers, reminds us that prisons can be daunting places, presenting potential challenges yet offering great rewards for anyone who chooses to work there. By using this premise in 2001, the University of Plymouth collaborated with a further education (FE) college prison education contractor, Strode College, and a Category C training prison, HMP Jasper.

The University had for a number of years educated and qualified teachers in the further education sector; those teaching young people and adults in colleges, work places, adult education centres and sixth form schools and colleges. The time had come to diversify.

During that academic year, a government bursary of £6,000 was introduced for all full-time student teachers, prompting a rise in demand for places on our programmes. At the same time, according to the Home Office (Communication Directorate, 2003), offender education was brought into the mainstream by placing it formally within the Department for Education and Skills (DFES) whilst having inspections carried out by the Adult Learning Inspectorate (ALI). With these elements coinciding, the time was ripe for developing the University's generic teacher education programme so that an element of it would have a specific focus on prisons.

After discussions with the Education Manager at HMP Jasper and his employer, Strode College, plans were made for recruiting students to the Cert Ed/PGCE programme where they could have their teaching placements in prison. In order to coordinate the students while teaching in prison, the University of Plymouth paid a fee per student to the education contractor for a Placement Coordinator to be employed.

Each applicant to the programme was invited for interview in HMP Jasper. For one or two candidates who had never been inside a prison before, experiencing bars on the windows and locked doors was so unnerving that their application was declined. This brief encounter with the prison regime was clearly essential for all potential students not only to experience the environment, but also to meet tutors and prisoners. Once accepted on the programme all the students were given a comprehensive course on security by prison officers.

Throughout all these programmes graduate and undergraduate students are taught together in the same group. The distinction between the PGCE and Cert. Ed. levels is made in the different assessed learning outcomes of the academic work. A typical full-time, one year Cert. Ed./PGCE programme consists of six modules; four core modules associated with teaching, learning, curriculum, theory and practice; and then two option modules. There is a choice of many option modules, among the most popular are: Psychology; Tutoring, Mentoring and Guidance; Information & Communications Technology (ICT), and Narrative Approaches to Practice.

In order for this programme to prepare the students for their specific teaching environment, the Education Manager at HMP Jasper wrote a module entitled, 'An Introduction to Tutoring within HMP Education Departments'. This took the place of one of the option modules. Two days each week were spent in lectures at the University and a third day for tutorials and directed study; the other two days were on teaching placement in the prison. Each student was assigned an experienced prison teacher as a mentor for guidance and support. To supplement resources in the University library and on the websites, books about prison were purchased for the group on placement to borrow.

Aims of the Programme

Many of the aims of the programme were mutually related to the three-way partnership:

- The University increased student numbers and widened participation. The development of the programme enabled our students and lecturers to develop their knowledge and understanding of a marginalised area of education.

- The Education Contractor fostered the skills of potential employees and enhanced the professionalism of those already teaching in prison. The student teachers assisted the prison teachers in a variety of curriculum areas and eventually helped to achieve Key Performance Targets in Literacy and Numeracy.
- The prison had a convenient group of enthusiastic teachers who could bring in new ideas and help to boost the numbers in the Education Department. They also raised the interest in education amongst staff and prisoners. Thus a culture of learning was promoted.

In addition, aspects of quality assurance were rigorously monitored by each of the three partners. The *Offender's Learning Journey* insists that, 'the quality of provision will reflect that generally found in the further education sector,' (DFES, 2004).

The major aim of education in prison is to help and encourage offenders to expand their knowledge and skills in order to nurture the process of rehabilitation and resettlement. In this sensitive education environment, where security is paramount, the systems and rules for teachers were emphasised but, as Palmer (1998) argues, effective teaching cannot be reduced to techniques, rather it relies on the integrity and the personality of the teacher. By this he means that the teacher, with a kind personality and a strong sense of personal identity, should be able to connect with the students and link them to the subject. Nellis (2002) has studied the autobiographies of reformed offenders who stress the importance in this process of staff who:

> ... treat offenders with dignity, who listen patiently, who respond constructively to emotional distress – in essence, staff who exhibit genuineness, warmth and empathy. (Nellis, 2002)

Humanistic philosophy such as this prevails throughout adult education; at the same time however, the teacher education programme was attempting innovation in an education sector that has been long overlooked. The *Offender's Learning Journey*, which describes itself as a blueprint for the new Offender Learning & Skills Service, extols the kinds of developments that the partnership programme aims for:

We need to see a transformational change in teaching practices that takes account of individual needs of offenders and offers a wide range of methods to stimulate and encourage participation. (DFES, 2004)

The Cert. Ed./PGCE also addressed the shortage of qualified teachers in the sector by attracting those who might not have otherwise considered teaching in prisons. For these student teachers it was expected that they use and develop their existing knowledge and skills in a diverse range of subjects from Skills for Life, to Access to Higher Education, to Parentcraft classes, such as 'Fathers Inside'. A spectrum of teaching methods, supported by learning theories, was promoted in our programme for the student teachers to try out in their practice. They taught in the Education Department, in the Therapeutic Community, in the Vulnerable Prisoners' Unit and elsewhere, as the Education Manager of HMP Jasper at the time explained:

> Using the Cert. Ed./PGCE placement scheme, we actually for the first time did something that we've been trying to do for years, that is have genuine support for education within workshops and out on the wings. That has meant we have specifically designed literacy packages around various workshop activities – and that has given us an enormous amount of KPTs.

These Key Performance Targets (KPTs) indicated the numbers of prisoners required to reach Entry Levels, Level One and Level Two in literacy and numeracy. The KPTs are set by the DFES for each Education Contractor who then allocates numbers for each prison. These targets were not intended to be an aspiration; they were set to be achieved.

Men and women of all ages were attracted to the programme from a broad background such as; lawyer, accountant, pub landlord, musician, policeman (who was concerned that he might be recognised), author, seaman, ex-prisoner, radio journalist and so on. Therefore they were able to offer a wide range of knowledge, skills and experiences in their classes. Ensuring that the teaching practice undergone by the each student was sufficiently stimulating and matched their skills was a challenge for the Placement Coordinator. For two students, this involved moving to another prison, HMP Drood, where they developed the Information, Advice and Guidance centre and set up a Job Club.

All the students were formally observed in their teaching practice by the Placement Coordinator, University lecturers, subject specialists and each other. These peer observations allowed students both to give and to receive support and advice about their teaching from a different perspective. It encouraged a broader understanding of a range of teaching in prison and the development of a mutual support network amongst the student teachers. Most seemed to rise to the challenge of teaching in a difficult environment and to enjoy themselves. One student teacher explained her feelings about interactions with the prisoners:

> Probably the most important factor, which makes for success, is our relationship with the students. We always try to make the sessions enjoyable and it is clear that the students are always pleased to see us – as we are them. We try to get to know the students individually so that each week we can ask "how's your daughter", or, "did you hear about your parole?", and so on. The students like to feel that we are interested in them, care about them, and respect them as individuals.

We believe that this empathetic notion of teaching is an essential element of effective student learning. At the end of the programme, some stayed at HMP Jasper to take up employment as qualified teachers, some went to other prisons, whilst others taught elsewhere. Many have become valued teachers within the prison education sector, at least two of whom have been recognised nationally:

> 1. For his work with the English Speaking Board, one of our past students won the Christian Churches Beacon Award for his employer Strode College. This teacher was outstanding in developing prisoners' aptitude for public speaking, enabling them to gain in self-confidence as well as increasing their ability to communicate lucidly. (PLSU, 2003).

> 2. Another of our past students was presented with the Butler Trust Award for initiating the 'Storybook Dads' scheme in a prison in 2002. The project has now spread to 23 prisons and young offenders' institutions. Prisoners write and read stories which are meticulously recorded on to a mini-disc. This is sent to their children, enabling the fathers to maintain family ties.

Storybook Dads was hailed by the Adult Learning Inspectorate as 'flying the flag for non-accredited learning'. (ALI, 2005).

Innovative ways of working with prisoners, such as these, was one of the aims of the teacher education programme. The Education Contractor from Strode College told me that one of his objectives was to try to help people to be more aware of prison education:

> I think it also recognises that prison education is part of a community just as much as a college or school is. Prisoners have got just as many needs and interests to be met as the people outside. A lot of those needs and interests are met through the education system and through the teachers who deliver it.

The programme was enhancing professionalism, introducing new ideas and raising awareness of prison education. It proved to be a great success but it was necessary to scan the horizon constantly to detect any possible trouble.

Troubleshooting

Some time into the programme most of the student teachers were issued with keys, rather than having to be escorted within the prison by a member of staff. This exemplified the trust shown by the prison security personnel who trained the student teachers to be acutely aware of how they interacted with the prisoners, particularly what was discussed, the words spoken, body language and the way they dressed. The Cert Ed/PGCE programme aroused the curiosity of the media, but they had only our students' security in mind, as the Education Manager recalled:

> When the television crew came here a few weeks ago, the only thing they were interested in asking me was, "Is it safe for these people?" ... It is safe as long as people have the right support, the right input, the right skills – then it's safe, but it isn't necessarily safe if you'd have none of that introduction to that environment.

These concerns were probably prompted by the news story at that time where a teacher in a prison in another part of the country had been taken hostage at knifepoint by a prisoner (Hook, 2001).

An unforeseen problem that created some disquiet among our students was the set holidays at the end of the University terms. As the Education Manager at HMP Jasper explained:

> Quite simply the department runs for 50 weeks a year, it's staffed for 50 weeks a year, staff schedule their holidays within that, and to have a group of students who have fixed holidays doesn't fit into that plan awfully well.

The situation was resolved by the cooperation of the students who either continued with their classes, staggered their holidays, or completed current work with their groups so that they could begin a new topic after the break.

These appeared as hiccups in a programme that was being well managed and supported by some influential people in the three partnership organisations. Any larger problems were circumvented at that time. Therefore, it was decided to expand the programme.

Building on Success

A group of students from another county was recruited to the full-time Cert. Ed./PGCE programme. As they all lived some distance from the University, the first module was run as a residential programme on the campus. For the rest of the course we had hoped to use Prison Service conference rooms just outside HMP Sapsea, but in the end rooms in a youth club were hired for contact sessions. The surroundings were clean, spacious and well-resourced, but isolated from both academic and professional interaction. Placements were organised in four different prisons and overseen by a second Placement Coordinator.

Both the variety of teaching practice locations: a local prison, two training prisons and a young offender institution, and the enthusiasm of the students rendered this a successful course. But, the unsatisfactory lecture rooms and the problems coordinating the widely distributed teaching placements halted plans for the formation of a second group. Nevertheless, the programme was satisfying its aim of recruiting new teachers to prisoner education when the Government issued new qualification targets for teachers in post-16 education, in a report *Success for All*: 'By 2010 we would expect that only new entrants to FE teaching would not be qualified.' (DFES, 2002). This edict compels all practising prison teachers, whether teaching academic or vocational subjects, to get a national teaching qualification.

When I asked an ALI prison inspector about staff development in education departments, he welcomed this new emphasis on teacher training. He told me:

> I really do feel that some people in prison education have long been forgotten in terms of development... especially those instructional officers and workshop supervisors that have been tucked away at the back of prison workshops.

So, further boundaries were crossed to start a part-time group of students who were already teaching in prison.

All Mixed Up Inside

On this occasion the course would be taught in a classroom inside HMP Jasper with a mixed group of uniformed and civilian staff as well as prisoners who taught their peers. This was a heady mix of students which could be potentially disastrous because "... the essential difference of adult education from all other kinds of education lies in its power relationships, the equality of the teacher and student participants – 'teaching all on equal terms'." (Rogers, 2002)

Yet in this classroom there was an imbalance of power ranging from the custodians to those in custody, from those with freedom to those without. Rogers (ibid.) argues that, 'Education which denies learners any power denies their adulthood'. Therefore, a priority for this group was to create at least a semblance of equality for all. The Placement Coordinator defined this objective of the course as the, '...them and us culture being gradually replaced by a culture of cooperation where offenders, teachers and prison staff work together as equal learners.' The divisive nature of this culture was explained to me by one of the prisoners on the programme: "Normally, whatever you do as an inmate – you're wrong. So, when the prison officers first joined they seemed to have an "I'm better than you" attitude. But, after a while they did give us plenty of encouragement."

It was not only the prisoners who felt uncomfortable at first. It took some brave decisions on the part of the staff, especially the prison officers, to relinquish some of their power and to expose themselves to possible ridicule by prisoners not in the class. For example, one prison officer was told, 'You're in a Noddy class with the inmates.' In addition, when a similar group was initiated in another prison, there was concern about the confidentiality of discussions between prisoners and staff that might occur in the sessions. Staff not participating in the programme feared that inappropriate classrooms discussions may cause a security risk. Some problems did occur, which will be described later, but it took some time and effort to overcome this initial prejudice and resentment.

The staff, who would always arrive first, left spaces between them around the tables for prisoners to sit, so that the whole group would be blended. Those prison officers in uniform would remove their epaulettes, so that to the untutored eye everyone looked not too dissimilar in appearance. This was confirmed when a Chinese scholar visited one of my classes; after we left he asked me, 'Who were the prisoners?' I was delighted as his question confirmed some achievement of my equality objective, although I never did tell my group. My colleague, another University lecturer, explained to me how she approached teaching her mixed group in the prison:

> From the start I tried to create a 'university space' within the confines of the venue ... it seemed to work with a willingness on both sides to minimise the difference. Creating their own ground rules and discussing boundaries first, aided this.

Everyone in the group was able to work together and learn from one another in a different setting, even though they were still in prison. The expectations of our aims and the academic tensions which arose about teaching such a diverse group, replicated the ongoing debates about the nature of adult education. For example, is it liberating in the sense that Freire (1973) advocated or could it be another form of domestication or social control argued by Coffield (1999)? Perhaps what we were doing was to find a path between these poles by emphasising the importance of working together in harmony. This idea is confirmed by Usher et al (1997):

> The purpose of education is less a matter of liberation or domestication than negotiating the terms of participation in a

learning process and a society in which subjection and autonomy co-exist.

Through this negotiation process, gradually the group began to develop an identity of its own. As my colleague told me, 'A kind of good-natured banter developed. They became close, I think because of the confines of the situation.' It is the fostering of this collective identity which Coare and Johnston (2003) argue is essential for creating a more productive and positive learning environment. For the prisoners this situation presented an opportunity to drop the identity of 'prisoner' and adopt the role of Higher Education student, something that could have lasting benefits:

Trying on a conformist identity in prison, as a purely cognitive process, is much easier than establishing the role commitments that will elevate the salience of this identity and guide behaviour on release... We believe that trying on the roles of productive citizen, responsible citizen and active citizen provides at minimum, an imaginative rehearsal for their assumption upon release. (Uggen et al, 2004)

Adopting or even testing a new identity, which is often an important factor in the notion of the transformative power of education, is a complex and contentious process. For example, Illeris (2003) argues that age plays an important part in facilitating learners to adopt a new identity because, 'Young adults view education as a central element of continuing identity development'. Whereas, he continues, older adults find it harder to discard parts of their old identity while attempting to develop a new one. The importance of this age factor might not be well supported, but every definition of learning involves the notion of change. Often this requires support and empathy from the teacher.

All participants benefited from the Cert. Ed./PGCE programmes, but it seemed that prisoners had most to gain through this potential process of transformation. This idea was expanded by the Placement Coordinator who explained:

In general for offenders the course is more about reflection, growth and changing attitudes. Participants have experienced increased confidence and feelings of self-worth. Indeed, one prisoner was so motivated that he turned down parole in order to complete the course.

This quote demonstrates the potency of the education programme, particularly for prisoners who are empowered to take responsibility for themselves and, at the same time, contribute to the teaching and learning of their peers.

Prisoners as Teachers

Many prisoners assist teachers in academic classes such as Skills for Life and ICT, as well as vocational classes such as Industrial Cleaning. It is not a soft option for a prisoner to teach his peers, as my University colleague explained, 'This was both challenging and rewarding for them as they were attempting to be in control in the classroom and then 'one of the lads' on the wings.' There is also, for example, a national peer-tutor scheme, *Toe-by-Toe* promoted by the charity The Shannon Trust, in which prisoners help their peers to read. This is gaining popularity and praise throughout the country (DFES, 2005; HoC, 2005). Perhaps the scheme would have even greater benefit to all if the peer tutors had the chance to gain teaching qualifications? As one ex-offender on our PGCE programme told me:

> I remember [in prison] writing letters for guys that I knew to their girlfriends. And I didn't know how to teach them, but if I did, I would have.

So there are many opportunities for prisoners to teach inside prison and to use the qualification gained to teach adults outside. Offenders are carefully interviewed, as are all applicants to the programmes, and the nature of their crimes considered before acceptance as a student. They are told that once qualified as a post-compulsory education teacher, there would be some restrictions on them, as ex-offenders, working with vulnerable people (DFES, 2002). Certainly at least two of the ex-offenders who have graduated from our programme are working as teachers, one as a lecturer in an FE college and one as a drug information worker. Despite our teachers qualifying to teach adults there is still a criticism of the course from, for example, the Head of Learning and Skills at HMP Jasper who argues that there is a 'lack of employment/progression routes for offenders who complete the programme and gain the Cert. Ed. or PGCE due to legal constraints on offenders in certain categories'.

This is a sensitive and complex problem, but it would be unethical to give people unrealistic expectations of career prospects. Despite this criticism, the programme where staff and prisoners study together to gain a teaching qualification was gaining an enviable reputation and, therefore, it grew.

Changing the Culture

A second course inside prison began in HMP Jasper and a new one started in HMP Sapsea. The teacher education programme was also adopted at HMP Cloisterham where there was less enthusiasm for a mixed group, so prison officers only applied. The Head of Learning and Skills (HOLS) at HMP Sapsea was especially pleased about recruiting all four Physical Training Instructors (PTIs) at the prison. After they had completed their Cert. Ed. qualification, they then studied two further modules in Teaching Literacy and Numeracy. These latter modules formed a specialist training qualification designated by the Government (DFES, 2003). This extensive study enabled the PTIs to enhance their practical teaching in the gym and to teach Skills for Life. The HOLS told me, 'This has created a pocket of excellence in the prison,' adding that the PTIs were truly embedding learning within the gym as well as in a separately equipped classroom where they could underpin the theory related to the taught practical skills. The HOLS believed that the education department tended to attract motivated learners, whereas the gym appealed to disaffected learners. Therefore by integrating education into the gym, a further swathe of learners was being encouraged with a new culture evolving. It was just this change of culture towards the natural acceptance of lifelong learning that was the priority for Helena Kennedy in her seminal report Learning Works. Here she advocated that: '"Learning Gain" should be on par with getting fit and just as ready a subject of conversation' (Kennedy, 1997).

This widening participation in learning continued the developing theme of innovative teaching where education was taken out of the department and into workshops where learning was related to the work done. Additionally, our student teachers went to the accommodation blocks to teach those prisoners who were reluctant to face entering a classroom. This form of outreach teaching came to be affectionately known as 'wing walking'. It has now evolved into specialised 'learning pods' on the wings where prisoners can be tutored in reasonable privacy. These so-called 'non-traditional' learners who are seen to both enjoy learning and to benefit from it are likely to become advocates for education, encouraging others who have yet to be attracted to study. So a self-perpetuating learning culture could be generated in every prison. This would not necessarily be restricted to the prisoners; in each course, prison staff from education, probation, the workshops, vocational training, kitchens and gardens were studying for their teaching qualifications. Everything was going almost too well.

Coming Apart at the Seams

One of the aspirations of this programme was to initiate a speciality prison where prsioners from elsewhere could apply to be transferred to HMP Jasper to study for a teaching qualification. There might be a dedicated study wing where prisoners could work in quiet surroundings. It was even hoped that the prison could become the first dedicated secure college, an idea that was espoused by Martin Narey, former head of the National Offender Management Service (NOMS). Now these hopes have been dashed since both the mixed students courses where prisoners studied with staff have been curtailed at HMPs Jasper and Sapsea.

A prisoner, who was described by the HOLS at HMP Sapsea as 'particularly manipulative', was visited on a Saturday by two staff members who were studying with him on the Cert. Ed./PGCE programme. Prison security considered this an inappropriate contact as, 'the relationship went beyond what was anticipated'. Consequently, the mixed group was disbanded by the Governor.

At HMP Jasper the HOLS wanted a formal Service Level Agreement from the education contractor and the University. This contract did not materialise partly because the HOLS, who recognised major benefits of the programme, also had some serious criticisms. He made a list which included the following:

- Some students and staff try to flex security requirements which can create tensions within the secure environment.
- The quality of the learning experience can be reduced for offender learners when teaching is undertaken by inexperienced students.

- Prison teacher time is taken up supporting Cert. Ed./PGCE students in the 'mentor role' which detracts from time available for experienced teachers to support and teach this group of learners.
- If teacher time is being purchased from the education contractor, and that teacher is mentoring or supervising a student, is the contract being delivered?
- There is a lack of clarity concerning academic assignments which have led to conflict when civilian students have sought to use their assignments to confront the custodial system rather than focusing on the educational aspects of learning in a secure environment.

However valid these criticisms may be, some of them attack the education contract, the concept of academic freedom and consequently the very nature of the cooperation required for the three-way partnership between the prison, the FE college contractor and the University to function. As no agreement could be reached, the mixed group was withdrawn by the contractor and the University. The prisoners could not continue with their studies, whereas other members moved to an outside location to carry on with the course.

Currently mixed groups of staff and prisoner Cert. Ed./PGCE learners have started at two new prisons in the region. HMP Sapsea is likely to start another mixed group of learners shortly. The awkward issues raised are being addressed, if not resolved. However, just as in the previous groups, all of the learners will study the specialist module, 'Introduction to Tutoring within HMP Education Departments'.

The Prison Education Module

This specialist module, which forms part of the Cert. Ed./PGCE programme, is worth 20 Credit Accumulation and Transfer (CATs) points at HE levels 1 and 3 respectively. Subject content includes the history, the nature and the role of education within prisons which is studied along with concepts of the curriculum, the teacher's professionalism, responsibilities, duties; and the education needs of the students. It was this module that made the generic academic programme a specialised Cert. Ed./PGCE for those wishing to teach, or already teaching, in prison.

As this was a unique venture, the Deputy Director of the Offenders' Learning and Skills Unit (OLSU) was invited to a meeting with representatives from the University of Plymouth, HMP Jasper and Strode College to discuss the structure of the teacher education programme and its future progress. As a result of this meeting it was decided to develop the module by seeking the views of various organisations associated with the education of prisoners, in order to incorporate some of these ideas into the module content. This was done with the encouragement of the OLSU, but it soon became clear that the module would be not only too large but also that the content could not satisfy all interested parties. Therefore, with the assistance of a teacher from a college in the north of England, who was running a lower level but slightly similar unit for teachers in prisons, the prison education module was finessed. The purpose of this refinement was to launch the module nationally so that everyone involved in teaching prisoners would have the opportunity of developing their knowledge and skills.

As it would be impractical for us to attempt to teach the module in every prison in the country, it was decided to cascade the teaching. A Master's module entitled, 'Education of Offenders: teaching and learning issues', was written and devised, as a cooperation between the University and Strode College, to incorporate a critical review of the specialist prison education module along with in-depth study of related topics. Participants, who successfully completed the assessed academic study, could choose to receive 30 CATs points at M level or a Certificate in Advanced Professional Studies (CAPS). As well as confirming their professional development, the qualification would entitle them to teach the Cert. Ed./PGCE specialist module in prison education. These courses, which are aimed at appropriately qualified staff associated with prisoner education, have attracted prison officers, education managers, teachers and HOLS. They studied on one of six dedicated courses held in venues around England. This was jointly funded by the OLSU and the DFES Standards Unit so that the cost to the student of the one-week long residential courses was nil. There were active contact sessions, participant presentations and expert outside speakers. All concerned were able to immerse themselves in exchanging understandings with other professionals from different parts of the service, which was invaluable. Currently some of the successful participants are teaching the specialist prison education module at Cert. Ed./PGCE level in their prisons throughout the UK.

Thus, a small step has been taken within a few years to raise the awareness of prisoner education nationally and to qualify those professionals involved. It is essential that these developments continue.

Conclusion

Enhancing the professionalism of teachers and instructors in prisons has, since our partnership began in 2001, attempted to raise interest in teaching offenders from both inside and outside the sector. The Secretary of State for Education in a response to a statement that teachers were leaving prison education asserted:

> In order to prevent further loss of staff from the profession and to help improve recruitment, the Government must ensure that the specialist role of teaching staff in prisons is properly recognised and rewarded... The Government agrees that teachers and trainers need appropriate training in order to teach offenders, and that this is a valuable role which needs to be properly supported. (Clarke, 2005)

Just a few years ago those who taught in prison were forgotten in a teachers' pay initiative and omitted from the newly-formed Learning and Skills Council brief (Bayliss, 2003). Since then the Government has invested more finances, accompanied by a greater interest in the sector. Many enthusiasts from an array of interested organisations have assisted in the success of the academic programmes for professional educators in prisons. Partnerships have both flourished and foundered as we experienced cooperation and goodwill, as well as teething problems and some misunderstandings with what we intended to achieve. These are being addressed. New networks of professionals who have experienced these prison education programmes are forming throughout the country. Now, the momentum begun with prison teacher education should continue to support the formation of a first class education service for all offenders.

Bibliography

Adult Learning Inspectorate (ALI) (2005); Unqualified Success. *Talisman – Supplement*, Issue 43, September. Coventry: Adult Learning Inspectorate.

Bayliss, P. (2003); Learning Behind Bars: time to liberate prison education in *Studies in the Education of Adults*, Vol. 35 No. 2 Autumn pp. 157 – 172.

Clarke, C. (2005); Government response to the House of Commons Education & Skills Committee Report – Prison Education. London: The Stationery Office. June. Cm. 6562.

Coffield, F. (1999); Introduction: lifelong learning as a new form of social control, in Coffield, F. (ed.) Why's the Beer always stronger up North? – Studies of Lifelong Learning in Europe, Vol.II, Bristol: Policy Press.

Communication Directorate (2003); Making the Right Choice: helping offenders quit crime - the story so far. London: Home Office.

Department for Education & Skills (DFES) (2002), Success for All: reforming further education and training. London: The Stationery Office.

DFES (2003), The Skills for Life Teaching Qualifications Framework: a user's guide. London: The Stationery Office.

DFES (2004); The Offender's Learning Journey. London: The Stationery Office.

DFES (2005); Government Response to the House of Commons Select Committee Report – Prison Education. London: The Stationery Office.

Freire, P. (1973); Pedagogy of the Oppressed. Harmondsworth: Penguin.

Hook, S. (2001), Lecturers still not safe inside Prisons. *Times Education Supplement*, 20 July. p.37.

House of Commons Home Affairs Committee (HoC) (2005), Rehabilitation of Prisoners: first report of session 2004-05 Vol 1. January. London: The Stationery Office.

Illeris, K. (2003); Adult education as experienced by the learners, in International Journal of Lifelong Education, Vol. 22 No.1 (Jan – Feb) pp. 13 – 23.

Kennedy, H. (1997); Learning Works: widening participation in Further Education, Coventry: Further Education Funding Council.

Nellis, M. (2002); Prose and Cons: Offender Auto/Biographies, Penal Reform and Probation Training, The Howard Journal, Vol. 41 No. 5 Dec. pp. 434 – 468

Owers, A. (2005); Rights Behind Bars: the condition and treatment of those in detention, Prison Service Journal, No. 158. March pp. 63 – 71.

Palmer, P. (1998); The Courage to Teach. San Francisco: Jossey-Bass.

Prisoners' Learning & Skills Unit (PLSU) (2003); College wins award for communication courses, Get Wise, Issue 3. Summer.

Rogers, A. (2002); Teaching Adults (3rd ed.). Buckingham: Open University Press.

Uggen, C; Manza, J & Behrens, J. (2004); Less than the average citizen: stigma, role transition and the civic reintegration of convicted felons, in Maruna, S. and Immarigeon, R. (eds.) After Crime and Punishment: pathways to offender reintegration, Cullompton: Willan Publishing.

Usher, R: Bryant, I. and Johnston, R. (1997); Adult Education and the Postmodern Challenge: learning beyond the limits. London: Routledge.

Distance Learning in Prison: Prisoner-Students' Perspectives

Emma Hughes

Every month, over two hundred prisoners in England and Wales apply to the Prisoners' Education Trust, a small London-based charity, seeking funds that will enable them to study through distance learning. Prisoners apply for funds to study a wide range of subjects, both vocational and academic, ranging from accounting to zoology, car maintenance theory to A-level history. On average, seventy-five per-cent of applications are successful.

The intention of this chapter is to provide an analysis of why prisoners choose to study through distance learning. After a brief consideration of the research methodology, I will begin by examining those factors that have motivated the prisoners to undertake education and distance learning in prison. This will be followed by a consideration of those factors that may actually serve to discourage prisoners from education. The chapter will conclude by reviewing those factors that have more specifically encouraged students to undertake distance learning as opposed to, or in addition to, prison-based education.

Whilst this study is specifically focused on distance learning, it necessarily extends to encompass prisoners' motivations for, and experiences of, prison education in general. Many of the students involved in this research have taken classes in their education departments and their route ways into distance learning must be seen in this context. Simply focusing on why the following student began distance learning would fail to convey the magnitude of his decision to undertake education in the first place:

Up until last year I had used drugs for 27 years, spent over 15 years in prison, no education, no qualifications, and I read my first book in prison when I was 27, couldn't even read properly until I was 27...this is my first time on education in prison, this sentence [at the age of 39] (E- 2 Interview).

Building up from the students' experiences, it will be seen that the research paints a picture of a complex interaction between 'push and pull' factors, which serve to encourage or discourage educational motivation and progress. Some factors are external to the prison environment, consisting for example, of an individual's past experiences as well as interactions with family and friends; other factors are internal to the prison, consisting of institutional factors and personalities encountered. Equally, the student's own emotional and psychological perspectives must also be taken into account. In examining these factors, it will be shown that research on distance learning and education has broader implications for our understanding of how a prison's culture and environment may serve to encourage or impede rehabilitation and constructive activity amongst its prisoners.

Research Methodology

From the outset, it was intended that this research would primarily focus on the perspectives of the prisoner-students themselves, contributing to the growing body of related work carried out listening to prisoners' voices (see, for example: Reuss, 1997; Wilson & Reuss, 2000; Hughes, 2000; Braggins & Talbot, 2003; Clarke et al., 2004). The study is qualitative in nature and, as such, aims to provide an in-depth understanding, rather than statistical analysis, of the motivations and experiences of prisoner-students engaged in distance learning study.

Questionnaires were distributed to all Trust-funded learners in nine selected prisons. These prisons are all adult prisons; eight are men's prisons, one is a woman's. The establishments cover a range of security classifications, from an open prison to a high security prison, and are spread geographically throughout the country. The students were guaranteed confidentiality and assured that their decisions whether or not to participate would in no way affect future funding. Seventy-four students returned questionnaires. The response rate at each prison varied on average between 45% and 72%.

Semi-structured, in-depth interviews were carried out with forty-seven of the student respondents. The interviews lasted an average of thirty minutes each and the majority of interviews were tape recorded and transcribed. The data collected from the interviews, as well as the questionnaires, was analysed using a modified from of grounded theorising (Brewer, 2000; Strauss & Corbin, 1998). Additional material has been gathered from sources such as education department reports on students' progress and interviews with education department staff.

Motivations for education

Although prisoners' self-described motivations for education have been considered in earlier research, many questions have been left unexamined. In particular, there has been no thorough exploration of the route that the students have taken into education. For example, what was their previous experience of education? Why have they begun education at this particular point of their sentence? Have they been in prison before and, if so, did they enrol in education then too?

In order to answer these questions, it becomes necessary to consider pre-prison experiences of education. In doing so, it becomes clear that far from being an academic 'elite', many of the distance learners had negative experiences of school when younger. Although there are students in the sample who enjoyed academic success, stories of leaving school without qualifications, and of truancy and expulsion, were commonplace.

The following statements act as important reminders that many of the students who took part in this study did not 'get along with school' when they were younger. Martin describes how he: "left school basically with nothing...and with me going into drugs at that age as well, my education just went sideways (E-2 Interview). Steve "was expelled for misbehaving...I don't like authority" he added (I-I Interview). One student explained that "School didn't interest me at all" (G-1 Interview), her comment representative of many others. Another reported: "I was bullied. I was told I was dyslexic. I have a lot of negativity in education" (G-3 Interview).

That a considerable number of the students in this sample did not like or enjoy school when they were younger means that the routes that these students took back into education as adults in prison will be informative. For those students who had previously truanted or been expelled, the transformation in attitude from rejecting education to applying for distance learning will be of particular interest.

Education prior to prison

Interestingly, some of the students who had not responded to education when younger had clearly begun to regret their lack of education prior to their criminal conviction. At least four interviewees had enrolled in adult learning centres in the community prior to their prison sentence. Still others reported that they had wanted to return to education but had found costs prohibitive or circumstances unsuitable. As one student explained: "being married with two children doesn't really give you any room for education" (C-8 Interview). Primary reasons cited for this developing interest in education were having no academic qualifications, and a frustration with 'dead-end' jobs, which is blamed on the lack of qualifications. That some of the students had already experienced motivation to restart their education, despite negative experiences of education in school, has significant implications for any research which seeks to measure a cause-effect relationship between undertaking education whilst in prison and reducing reoffending. One must question whether it is simply the acquiring of skills or knowledge that may affect an outcome, or whether more complex motivational processes must be taken into account as well.

Given the above, it is not surprising that some of these interviewees turned directly to education in prison for the reason that: "Studies were already on my mind." Although this statement was made by one of the two interviewees who were involved in graduate level study at the time of their arrest, this statement can equally be applied to those who had regretted missed educational opportunities in the past. Prison in such cases can be seen as a "time-out" (C-8 Interview) and a "perfect opportunity" to be taken advantage of with respect to education.

However, whilst some of the students turned to education for reasons originating in pre-prison experiences, the remaining students' motivations were more directly affected by in-prison experiences and/or the acquiring of a criminal record, with its implication for post-release futures, as shall be shown below.

Turning to education in prison

Approximately half of the students interviewed began education, whether through education departments or distance learning, shortly after coming into prison. In some cases this meant whilst still on remand, in other cases, shortly after being convicted. No specific time limit will be assigned to this notion of 'right away', a phrase that is specifically used by some interviewees. However, this notion will be used to set up a more general contrast between the experiences and decisions of those who turned to education earlier in their sentence, and those who waited until later in their sentence, or indeed, until a later sentence.

Regardless of when education is embarked upon, there are typically multiple motivations cited by students and it does not necessarily follow that the reason why education was begun was the reason why it was continued. This is evident, for example, in the sometime differing motives for starting on distance learning as opposed to prison-based education. The following should be interpreted, therefore, as providing insight into the general motivations and processes at work, rather than a definitive account of each individual's motivational histories, should such a thing be even a possibility.

Prison as an "eye-opener"

For some of the prisoner-students interviewed, it is prison itself that prompts a re-evaluation of one's attitude towards education as part of a larger process of reassessing one's life and future direction. The criminal conviction or prison sentence is effectively seen as a 'turning point.' In this vein, interviewees talked of prison as an "eye-opener" and of "needing to sort myself out" (D-4 Interview), and education is seen as an opportunity through which to achieve this end. As Keith explains: "I don't want to carry on how I lived my life in the past... the only way I can do that is really to learn, to get educated and to get some qualifications" (C-1 Interview). Joan, who did not like school when younger, says that her views on education changed after seeing other prisoners being released, but returning soon after: "When you have a decent education behind you and apply for jobs and things like that you're not so stuck on the out" (G-1 Interview).

Concern for the future

Regardless of when a decision to enrol on education was taken, unquestionably, the primary motivator cited for education in prison was future related. Whilst some interviewees talked more generally of trying to ensure a 'brighter future,' overwhelmingly, the talk of the future revolved around issues of finding employment. As Scott puts it: "I don't want to be out of work when I go out" (B-4 Interview). Significantly, this concern with employment prospects was shared both by those with successful employment and educational records, and those without. There is a common concern that given their criminal conviction and time spent in prison, finding employment will be difficult. There is, however, a belief that education in prison will "give you a better chance to move on for when you're outside" (H-1 Interview).

Education is essentially seen by the students as contributing to employment prospects in two different but complementary ways. Firstly, education is seen as giving one the skills and qualifications required for a specific job, or jobs in general. Secondly, education is used by the students in an attempt to counter their prison record.

In regards to gaining skills and qualifications, it is frequently the desire to prepare for a certain type of job that motivates an application for distance learning, as opposed to study within an education department. The students typically take into account the potential limitations imposed by their criminal records on employment options and this is also reflected in their selection of courses. Computer-related courses are popular with the students, in part because it is felt that they could lead to employment in spite of criminal convictions. Business start-up courses are popular amongst the students because self-employment is seen as a good alternative. Other factors taken into account when considering job prospects include the availability of jobs in a particular line of work, previous work or educational experience, and expected age at release. Andy, for example, has taken Coastal Navigation and Coastal Skipper/Yachtmaster Offshore theory courses since being in prison. He writes that:

> For many years I was employed as a boat builder, and served my time in various boatyards, but I had not been able to own my own boat, and more importantly learn the skills required to take one to sea. I do now own a small sailboat, and will again after my release, and I saw this as an ideal opportunity to study the courses available to me. It will also open up a new avenue for me on release, as I will have a recognised skill to offer, which even today appears to hold no age bar. (H-2 Questionnaire)

In an effort to counter their criminal record, students may use education to demonstrate that time in prison has been used constructively, as a way of indicating that they have 'changed', and to increase their qualifications in comparison to other potential applicants. In this respect, the opportunity to undertake more advanced level study is thought of as crucial, even amongst those who started with no qualifications. This in itself is another significant factor in explaining why the interviewees have turned to distance learning. As Jason, studying accounting through distance learning puts it: "[my studies will] give me better opportunity than most" (A-2 Interview).

This notion of gaining more options is often related to a desire to "better oneself," or as Eric explained: "I knew I had to do something with the rest of my life and I wanted to make it as successful as I could" (C-8 Interview). In making such statements, some of the interviewees seek to distinguish between themselves and many of their fellow prisoners with interesting implications for concepts of self-identity and self-esteem. As one student points out: "there's a lot of people in prison who don't want to better themselves, they just go to their jobs...they're not going to change their normal progress through the system" (C-1 Interview). Another student states: "Well, I'm sorry to say but there are a lot of people in prison that there's just no hope for" (C-8 Interview). This concept of the 'no-hoper', however, will be returned to later on. Some of the distance learners in this sample may previously have been seen to fit such a description; what led to a change in their "normal progress through the system" will be examined.

Concern for the future is clearly a primary motivator for education and distance learning in prison, but there are still more pieces of the puzzle missing. How, for example, did some of the students discover their interests? How did some of those with no qualifications progress to distance learning? What of those prisoners not immediately thinking in terms of future employment?

Education as a response to prison experiences

In a number of cases, the students initially turned to education as a response to their immediate surroundings and circumstances. The idea of "doing something" through education, a phrase that echoes throughout the students' accounts, can be seen as being in contrast to doing 'nothing' in other areas of the prison. Prison workshops in particular are singled out as being unproductive and mundane. Scott describes how the other prisons in which he had been held "didn't have education and you were sitting 'round all day doing nothing, sitting in the 'shops all day" (B-4 Interview). Likewise, Patrick, who had offered computer training to other employees as part of his pre-prison employment, undertook education in prison:

> Because there is little else to do which offers any meaningful structure to your life. You can go to work, but if you've got education you can at least organise your life so that you're making some progress, especially if you've got a long time to go. The vast majority of work that's available doesn't offer a great deal to challenge- it's repetitious and mundane work (B-3 Interview).

Avoidance of boredom was also cited as a motivation for undertaking education amongst those who had previously disliked school and who did not hold high expectations for what education might deliver. Trevor, who came into prison with no qualifications, reports that: "[I] had to do education or some sort of work in the mornings, so I chose to do education... it was either that or mop floors." Education was, he explains: "just to kill my boredom, really, to start with" (F-6 Interview). Likewise, Kevin enrolled in education in prison because, "to be honest, at that stage it was either go behind your door or do some education classes. I thought why not, get out my cell, I'll have a go at something and so I did. I did some basic English and RSA certificates" (E-6 Interview). How motivation for education that is rooted in avoidance of boredom might potentially transform into the pro-active decision to apply for funding for distance learning will be explored in due course.

However, the offerings available within the education department clearly affect whether this decision to turn to education is made, especially amongst those beyond basic skills. Scott compares his experience of the training prison he is currently in to the prisons and Young Offender Institution (YOI) that "didn't have education." The YOI was aimed, he clarifies, at basic education, and having already gained GCSEs, he felt there was nothing for him. He began education at the training prison "where there were more educational opportunities, like science and music theory" (B-4 Interview). He went on to take a creative writing course through distance learning and became deputy editor of his prison's magazine.

Access to information about the educational possibilities that exist is clearly vital for encouraging new interests to develop. Steve left school at age fourteen without qualifications. Like others in the sample, he became frustrated with workshop offerings and decided, "working on Walt Disney lampshades was not for me" (I-1 Interview). He also wanted "to do something useful" that would provide some "self-satisfaction". He found that satisfaction doing copy typing into Braille, a work programme based in the education department. Of significance, his exposure to the education department "opened up scope" as he saw "what was going on". From a start point of seeking out something "useful", that did not necessarily involve education, he found himself seeking the education manager's advice about doing "something that will benefit me when I get out" and from there, with her encouragement, began the first of many courses, mostly through distance learning.

Prison-based experiences were likewise a significant factor for many of the students taking distance learning courses related to counselling skills (the most popular subject choice amongst this sample and related to the most popular employment interests). For some, it was the experience of undergoing counselling, in particular for drug and alcohol addictions, which introduced a desire to learn more about counselling. In other cases, it was the experience of being a Samaritan-trained Listener that encouraged the interest. Informatively, it was sometimes the experience of having been 'listened' to by other prisoners when they first entered prison that initiated this interest:

When I was first on remand, there was a great, big old chap who was a Listener and I sat a couple of hours, once or twice, sat in his cell pouring my heart out to him and he was excellent and I thought that was really good and when I got to ____Prison I thought, yeah, I'd accepted my sentence by now and I thought well, he helped me through that and I thought yes, if I can do the same for somebody else then I'll do it. (E-1 Interview).

Mike was similarly inspired to be a Listener after being 'listened' to. He describes how this in turn led to his distance learning study:

I thought 'well I'll try this counselling [course]…'cause I have been trained to be a Listener when I was in _____ Prison, so I think that encouraged me more when I passed to be a Listener to do something for like helping other people and that's what the counselling does (A-1 Interview).

The story of Mike, who has experienced a long-term struggle with addiction and has served numerous prison sentences, will be returned to later on for it touches upon many of the factors that can hinder educational development. However, in referring to the encouragement that he received from "pass[ing] to be a Listener," Mike highlights the role that growth in self-confidence can play in a prisoner's decision to begin education.

Other students in the sample reported enrolling in education only after gaining self-confidence, particularly in their academic ability, whilst in prison. The initial lack of confidence goes some way to explaining some of the interviewees' delayed start to education. Ed explains how:

I had been given a job in the laundry and when I was over there I immediately started to be given the jobs that other people weren't doing. I began to think that maybe I did have some 'grey matter' and maybe I could use it and since then I started taking education. That was basically why (D-1 Interview).

Ed has since completed key skills education classes, has served as editor of his prison's magazine, is an education orderly and is currently taking, through distance learning, an AS-level in Sociology and a computer course.

Taken together, the above examples provide insight into how decisions to undertake education can be motivated by confidence building experiences and exposure to new programmes and interests. The personalities encountered in prison, be they of education officers, prison officers, or other prisoners, can be instrumental in this regard.

Disincentives for education in prison

Whilst the findings presented above provide significant evidence of the prisoners' motivations for educational classes and distance learning in prison, the analysis is not complete. First, it potentially paints too linear a picture of progression into education. Second, it fails to address the obstacles and hindrances that may delay or even prevent educational enrolment altogether.

Not all of the students in the sample met with educational success or achievement during their first exposure to education in prison. Others spent many years in prison, on a number of sentences, before deciding to start education. Much can be learnt from their experiences. Furthermore, all of the students interviewed were specifically asked why other prisoners may choose not to undertake education. While in some sense the very fact of this question helped in the construction of an 'us versus them' narrative, the responses are informative on several levels. In responding to the question, some of the students referred to their own initial reluctance to undertake education in prison as well as to their perceptions of other peoples' reluctance.

Gathered from these varied perspectives, the disincentives for education referred to by students will be examined below. Continuing the investigation from the preceding section, psychological outlooks, institutional influences, and the personalities of those encountered, will all be seen to play a potential part in whether a prisoner enrols in education.

Personal factors that may discourage education

The role that increased self-confidence may play in encouraging educational involvement has already been considered. It is also telling that the prisoner-students consistently cited lack of confidence as one of the primary reasons why fellow prisoners might not in enrol in education:

> The majority of the reason I think is lack of confidence. That's one big thing. The majority of people that are in here have come from council estates. They're very similar to me. They didn't do that well at school, you know, and they don't think they could do it. If you don't think you can do something, a lot of people don't want to try. It's just the fear of failure isn't it? (B-1 Interview).

Further illustrating the point above, Aaron, who serves as a peer tutor, tells how:

> There's a lad on my wing, a young cleaner, and he's opted to become a cleaner. He can't read and write. I've been taking home work home and we've been secretly going back to his cell and he's been going through these Beginner worksheets, not even Entry Level, because he literally can't read and write, all he can write is his own name, and that's a bit wobbly. But he's too scared to come up to education... *(E-1 Interview)*.

Against this backdrop, the confidence boosting experiences described in the preceding section, take on even greater significance.

For some prisoner-students, their decisions regarding education cannot be understood without reference to underlying drug and alcohol addictions. Addictions may serve to undermine educational motivations and progress, whilst treatment of such addictions may allow an interest in education to develop. As examples below shall attest, successful treatment of drug and alcohol addictions whilst in prison can play a crucial role in transforming those that may have been described as 'no-hopers' into pro-active students seeking funding for distance learning.

Bill has, in his own words, "been coming in and out of prison for a number of years now," and has "had a drug problem for 14 years" (E-4

Interview). Of previous sentences he says: "I've never really done anything with my time in prison, just sat in my cell, I've done nothing basically" (E-4 Interview). He had attended some education classes during a previous sentence, but as he explains: "it was more for, well just to get out. It was an easy option...I didn't really sort of put any effort in, didn't take any exams or do anything" (E-4 Interview). He offers the following insight on why things are currently different:

> With this sentence my perspective on myself and my life has changed tremendously but that's also through the course that I'm doing on the Drug Therapeutic Community [in which he lives]. With regards to the [distance learning] course, I would say that it's been a part of the process within the TC as well. This whole sentence for me has been a really good learning experience (E-4 Interview).

For students like Bill, education may be seen as a means through which to achieve new "goals and aims" (E-4) once the addiction is no longer an overriding factor. He talks of wanting to go to college and of "want[ing] something better and one of the ways of doing that for me was to start to get an education. Start to build back what I'd lost all those years ago when I started playing truant from school and things like that (E-4 Interview).

Mike is a self-described 'career criminal' who has spent much of his life in prison. His experiences, detailed below, indicate how educational interest might develop out of a combination of interrelated factors, including drug addiction treatment, growth in self-confidence, and exposure to new interests. His decision to become a prison Listener was considered in the previous section. However, his story also cautions against the creation of the aforementioned linear picture of progression within education:

> ...it was the beginning of my sentence in '94 that I got interested in the education side of things because I never really went to school when I was outside you see. I've always been a criminal near enough all my life so I used to bunk off school a lot...I thought that while I'm in prison it would give me an opportunity to learn more about education, some maths, English and other subjects that might come up (A-1 interview).

Mike began taking education department classes. But, as he explains:

> I got involved with all the drugs and things again so my head was back where it was when I first came to prison you know, and then I was in segregation units. In and out of segregation units all the time... I decided just to forget it all you know (A-1 Interview).

He was "in a segregation unit for about two years and I was away from everybody else and then I sort of began to look at my life, my past life, my past criminal lifestyle and I thought I would do something. Then I got released from the segregation unit and I went back onto normal allocation and then I thought 'well I'll try this counselling...'cause I have been trained to be a Listener when I was in _____ Prison, so I think that encouraged me more when I passed to be a Listener to do something for like helping other people and that's what the counselling does (Interview with A-1).

Mike subsequently transferred to a prison where he could engage in intensive therapy himself. As Mike concluded, acting as a counsellor is "something I've been interested in for a long time, but like I say in the criminal lifestyle when I was outside, I really wouldn't bother but I think what I do now has always been there in me but this has just enhanced it more and I'm gonna continue with it" (A-1 Interview). Since the interview, he has completed the course he was taking, continued on to another prison, and begun a further distance learning course on counselling. He joked that he is now called "Counsellor" by fellow prisoners.

Whilst it is clear in the above examples that education was being hampered by untreated addictions, the larger questions as to why, at this point, the prisoners are addressing their addictions, and what one described as his "life style problems", are much harder to answer. Such questions form the backbone of research on desistance from crime as well treatment of addictions (cf: Maruna, 2001; Sampson & Laub, 2003; Miller & Heather, 1998) and go beyond the scope of this chapter. However, it is worth noting that some of the students have equated their change in perspective with the fact that they are "getting older now;" and have a desire, as Mike put it, "to do something." Martin, who has spent more than fifteen years of his life in prison, and who had until this sentence used drugs for 27 years, refers to the fact that he is "turning the big 40" as reason for wanting, like Mike, "to do something" (E-2 Interview). He, too, would like to work as a counsellor and is taking relevant courses through distance learning.

Whilst keeping in mind what has been referred to as the "...extensive relapse and recycling [which] occurs across the population of addicted individuals who are attempting to take action to stop the behaviour" (DiClemente & Prochaska, 1998, p. 6) it becomes apparent that education is offering these students the chance that they seek "to do something." Their successful application for distance learning courses is evidence that something is actually being done. In this respect it is also of interest to note Maruna's (2001) observation that working in the counselling field "seems to be an increasingly popular path for former deviants who desist from crime and drugs" (p. 102) and that a desire to help others and to achieve something is typical of the narratives of those ex-offenders who successfully desist from crime.

Prison-based factors that may discourage education

Up until now, the factors described as potentially disrupting or impeding the uptake of education are rooted in personal issues; the following two factors to be addressed, reduced wages for education and limited curricula, are rooted in the institutional environment itself. Whilst not the only de-motivators identified within this context, these two were the most frequently cited.

The students consistently referred to the lower wages paid to prisoners on education, in comparison to the wages paid in workshops, as a significant disincentive for enrolling on education. Whilst recent developments have seen adjustment of pay to bring education in line with workshops in some establishments, this is not yet the case in all prisons. In one prison for example, at the time of interview weekly wages in the kitchens could earn one up to £14, whilst the maximum paid for education was £5.90 (E-1 Interview). Larger discrepancies were reported elsewhere. Taylor (2004) provides details of the wage variation currently existing.

Given the considerable impact that wages can have on a prisoner's life, it is not surprising that this may be seen as a disincentive. Reduced wages may equate, for example, with less phone cards with which to contact family and friends, and for those who smoke, less tobacco. Those prisoners without external financial assistance from family and friends may be further discouraged from education.

As one student commented: "Prison wages for education are the main reason people stay away from enrolling" (J-5 Questionnaire). Another suggested: "The people who need education [do] not get it as they can't be bothered. They should pay more to those who do education. Then they might help some to do it" (H-1 Questionnaire). Referring to those students who harbour a fear of education, a distance learner points out: "if you get a job in the workshops, you can get more money that way. So why bother?" (C-2 Interview).

The wage discrepancy has led some students to question the value that prison administrators place on educational endeavour, and by extension, rehabilitation. "The prison reduces your pay for bettering yourself with education," remarked one prisoner (H-5 Questionnaire). Another complained that education: "is still seen by many staff as a 'soft option' to real prison work- this seems to be reflected in the pay disparity- educationalists being obviously penalised by a big reduction in pay" (H-8 Questionnaire).

Other concerns voiced by the students revolved around the limited curricula available in education departments. Education staff are frequently praised for encouraging education, however, there is a common view that the restricted curricula and the focus on basic skills serve to turn prisoners away. This is noted both by those who came into prison with qualifications, as well as those who earned their first qualifications whilst in prison, but feel that they have no way to progress. Whilst courses are available in all prisons through the Open University (OU), to be eligible one must first have completed an introductory course (for which outside funds are generally needed), and university level study might not be suitable for all those looking to continue their studies.

One student remarked: "The education department in this prison is very helpful but I do think that if [there was] more funding and availability of resources... then more inmates would choose to re-educate themselves" (E-4 Questionnaire). Said another: "If your requirements are anything other than basic, prison has nothing to offer" (J-2 Questionnaire).

It was to fill the perceived vacuum that many in the sample turned to distance learning. However, seeking funds and the opportunity to further one's study may not always be easy. Students were not always aware of funding options and others talked of encountering "problems" and "obstacles" when they tried to continue their studies beyond the levels offered in their prison. One student stated: "It can be a struggle to gain further education. I was surprised that you need to find the funds yourself as I would have thought it to be part of one's rehabilitation" (F-7 Questionnaire). The need to be "determined" in one's pursuit of such goals reoccurs, and suggests a level of self-confidence that might be required, even just to submit an application for funds.

Discouragement of education by others

A final factor to be considered as a possible de-motivator for education is rooted in the prison environment but consists not of regime or regulations, but of the personalities of those encountered, including other prisoners and staff. Whilst a recurring theme in the research is the encouraging role played by other prisoners in terms of educational achievement and progress, it is worthwhile to note that several students referred to what one lifer describes as the "sort of unofficial prison politics that comes in" which may dissuade some people from taking classes:

> ...you will get some lads looking at you and it's 'oh, you go for education, why don't you come down with us to the workshop and like, play cards, play scrabble and drink tea. You may whack a few tables out, or sew a pair of jeans together or whatever, but be with the crowd, be with the mates and [just] pretend you're not in prison (E-10 Interview).

Aaron adds that: "There's some peer pressure in some areas, like you get a group of prisoners and they're like 'Oh, you don't want to get involved in that, it's girlie or whatever to go down to Education...so peer pressure plays a part in it" (E-1 Interview).

Not all prisoners reported such experiences, and variation was noted by establishment. A student in a prison holding a large percentage of lifers talked of the encouragement generally given to people seeking out new interests to help do their time. Prisoners housed on Vulnerable

Prisoner Units and Therapeutic Communities also typically reported an environment where fellow prisoners are more encouraging of education.

Nevertheless, it is helpful to consider the effect that general attitudes towards education within a prison, and not exclusively belonging to prisoners, might have on a prisoner's decision of whether or not to pursue education. After all, Charlie recounts how some prison officers convey the belief that: "the workshop [is] where you should be- you shouldn't have education" (E-10 Interview). His comment echoes reports elsewhere of anti-education attitudes among some prison officers, particularly when it comes to more advanced level study (see, for example, Reuss, 1997; or Worth, 1996). Another distance learner describes how he and other prisoners are called names by the officers, "stupid" and "useless" amongst them. He argues: "after a number of times you may begin to believe it" (D-1 Interview). Given the low self-confidence reported by this student and others, such remarks may be seen as all the more troubling.

However, these comments are thrown into further relief through juxtaposition with the following statement illustrating the positive impact that prison staff can have on the encouragement of educational endeavour:

> The officers are always encouraging me, makes me feel a lot better. It makes me more determined to pass. Sometimes people say 'good' and then sometimes they say 'you're brilliant, girl'. They're saying it and sometimes they say things that you don't see…Officers here like when you are determined to do things like change you life, they come up and try to help (G-2 Interview).

Such assistance can play a vital part in helping to offset self-doubts and other personal and institutional deterrents that a prisoner may be experiencing.

A Summary: Why distance learning?

In concluding this chapter, it is helpful to focus specifically on some of the students' reasons for undertaking distance learning as opposed to, or in addition to, education department based classes. Explanations of such decisions have already surfaced though the course of the preceding sections on motivations and disincentives for education in prison, but a refocus on them will serve to reiterate some of the themes that have emerged so far.

In the material that has been presented, there have also been indications of some of the benefits that prisoners may derive from education and distance learning, such as enjoyment, increased self-confidence, expansion of interests, preparation for the future, and what one student has described as a sense of "hope and direction" (B-3 Questionnaire). More detailed exploration of the benefits that students have described is offered elsewhere (Hughes, 2000; Hughes, 2004). However, for current purposes, it should be noted that these benefits can themselves be encouraging of further educational study, which for some students includes making a transition to distance learning.

Limited curricula, is not surprisingly, a common reason put forth for undertaking of distance learning: "I've done everything I could here and they couldn't offer me anything else..."(C-7 Interview) explains one distance learner. Another student chose to take education classes immediately after arriving in prison, but completed all the prison-based courses within two to three months, and still had an estimated three years to serve. As he put it: "then it's like, 'what next'?" (F-1 Interview).

Distance learning is also chosen because it allows students to pursue particular interests: "Well, my main thing was languages, doing languages. Unfortunately they stopped them so that's why I do distance learning" (C-7 Interview). There is also recognition that distance learning allows prisoners to pursue prospective employment interests that could not be catered for within education departments.

Illustrative of several of the motivators commonly described are those referred to by Will, who entered prison with some qualifications, although he "didn't think much of [education]" when in school. Although Will was training in landscape gardening/ conservation work through the National Trust when sent to prison, he would like to work in future with animals. He has a particular interest in "herpetology- snakes and reptiles-and things like that..." (E-9 Interview) and would like to pursue a degree in zoology at university. Through reading BBC Wildlife magazines he found out about related correspondence courses. He sent off for a prospectus and selected a course on Animal Behaviour. He secured funding from the

Prisoners' Education Trust at the recommendation of his education department.

Will does not attend prison education department classes, and has a full-time job elsewhere in the prison. He explains:

> I wanted to do education, but for one thing, alright, the money in here [for education] isn't all that good. What I'm doing now is about £10 per week but if you go on education it's about a fiver. And one thing, I wanted to keep the money as well as keep getting educated, so I said I'd do [distance learning] plus there's nothing in the prison that I wanted to do (E-9 Interview).

The final example touches upon similar ideas, but is also informative for highlighting the role that other distance learners may play in informing prisoners of the options for distance learning. Trevor had come into prison with no qualifications, and had initially gone into education because "it was either that or mop floors" (F-6 Interview.)

Discovering an interest and enjoyment in learning, he went on to complete all the courses in his education department. He speaks with pride of his achievements. "I've finished full-time education," he explains. "I've done a few extra courses that they had available. I've completed every course I've done except for Cooking which is just a new one - I've completed them all" (F-6 Interview).

Trevor was introduced to distance learning by another prisoner after he had completed full-time education and was working in the gym:

> Well, at the time, I wanted to get something that was going to benefit me in what I wanted to do when I get out. I wanted to get into the music industry, but I didn't want to get into it, like making actual music. I wanted to do the promoting, the producing, the directing, stuff like that. The course came up. It was introduced by [another prisoner]...he introduced me to the course and said it would be a very good basic introduction to start with. So that's what made me do that and the fact that I'd finished everything here. At the time, I still wanted to learn more things, so I opted to do that (F-6 Interview).

In conclusion, it is evident that prisoners' decisions as to whether or not to undertake education in prison, or distance learning in particular, may be the product of a vast array of factors potentially serving to encourage or discourage such courses of action. Past experiences (including school experiences), psychological states and personal matters, institutional procedures and regulations, programmes and activities offered in prisons, and the influences of individuals encountered, all have a role to play in this respect. An understanding of these factors, especially of those that may serve to deter educational undertaking in prison, is crucial if steps are to be taken to maximise the possibilities for prisoners to engage in constructive, and potentially transforming, activities in prison.

Bibliography

Braggins, J. & Talbot, J. (2003); Time to Learn: Prisoners' Views on Prison Education. London: Prison Reform Trust

Brewer, J. D. (2000); Ethnography. Buckingham: Open University Press

Clarke, A. et al. (2004); Delivering Cognitive Skills Programmes in Prison: a Qualitative Study. Home Office Research Findings No. 242, London: Home Office.

DiClemente, C. & Prochaska, J. (1998); Toward a Comprehensive, Transtheoretical Model of Change: Stages of Change and Addictive Behaviors, in W. R. Miller & N. Heather (Eds.), Treating Addictive Behaviors. (2nd ed.), New York: Plenum Press

Hughes, E. (2000); An Inside View: Prisoners' Letters, in D. Wilson & A. Reuss (Eds.), Prison(er) Education: Stories of Change and Transformation. Winchester: Waterside Press.

Hughes, E. (2004); Free to Learn? Prisoner-Students' Views on Distance Learning. Mitcham: Prisoners' Education Trust.

Maruna, S. (2001); Making Good: How Ex-Convicts Reform and Rebuild Their Lives. Washington DC: American Psychological Association.

Miller, W. R. & Heather, N. (1998); Treating Addictive Behaviors, (2nd ed.). New York: Plenum Press.

Reuss, A. (1997), Higher Education and Personal Change in Prisoners, unpublished Ph.D. dissertation, University of Leeds: School of Sociology and Social Policy.

Reuss, A. (1999); Prison(er) Education, The Howard Journal of Criminal Justice, 38 (2): 113-127.

Sampson, R. J. & Laub, J. H. (2003); Desistance from Crime over the Life Course, in J. T. Mortimer & M. J. Shanahan (Eds.), Handbook of the Life Course. New York: Kluwer Academic/ Plenum Publishers: 295-309.

Strauss, A. & Corbin, J. (1998); Basics of Qualitative Research: Techniques and Procedures for Developing Grounded Theory. London: Sage.

Taylor, S. (ed.) (2004); Directory of Offender Education 2005. London: Forum on Prisoner Education.

Wilson, D. (2000) Introduction, in D. Wilson and A. Reuss (Eds.); Prison(er) Education: Stories of Change and Transformation, Winchester: Waterside Press.

Wilson, D. (2001) Valuing Prisoner Education: The Establishment of the Forum on Prisoner Education, Prison Report: 18-19.

Wilson, D. & Reuss, A. (eds.) (2000); Prison(er) Education: Stories of Change and Transformation. Winchester: Waterside Press.

Worth, V. (1996); Supporting Learners in Prison, in R. Mills & A. Tait (Eds.); Supporting the Learner in Open and Distance-Learning. London: Pitman Publishing.

Do improved basic skills help the ex-prisoner after release?

Claudia Gosse

> We have put in place measures to improve offenders' educational attainment and improve their chances of securing work. ... Prison and probation services together share a priority to give adult offenders the chance to make up lost time on basic skills.
> *(David Blunkett, Reducing Crime - Changing Lives 2004)*

As a teacher of basic literacy in the Learning Centre of HMP Winchester I became aware of the fact that while most of the prisoner-students that passed through my class felt improved basic skills would help them in their personal and daily lives, few related them to enhanced employment or further education opportunities on release, indicating a discrepancy between Government views on prisoner education at this level and the views of learners themselves. In order to gain a better understanding of the basic skills prisoner-student beyond the classroom I obtained authorisation, in 2004, to follow up for six months on a small number of offenders leaving prison with new basic skills accreditation. The aim of the project was to assess the impact of basic skills gained in prison on the lives of ex-prisoners, and on their employment and further education opportunities. Regular interviews with participants over the six-month study period gave an insight into the resettlement difficulties faced by ex-prisoners, and how these influenced their ability to exploit and build on their improved basic skills. The full report on this research took the form of an MA (Ed) dissertation. The aim here is to give voice to the four participants who gave their time and spoke so openly about their lives and aspirations on release.

'Top of the ladder, then knocked back down'

All prisoner-students at HMP Winchester (Category B local prison), and HMP Camp Hill (Category C training prison), being released on licence into the Hampshire area in May and June 2004 with new basic skills accreditation, were invited to participate in the project. Of the six that agreed to take part, four remained on board at the end of the study period. All names have been changed. Through telephone and recorded face-to-face interviews the participants spoke of their expectations for resettlement, their hopes for the future and their perspectives of events as they unfolded. Being participant led, the number and length of interviews varied according to the individual, but some structured questionnaires were completed in order to provide a comparable basic profile of each participant and their aims. Dave, Garry, Kevin and Shaun were typical of the shorter-term prisoner that makes up the majority of the prison population, commonly referred to as 'the churn', and with some reservations they were all largely positive about their experience of basic skills education in prison:

> 'Helped remind me what I could do.' (Dave)

> 'I know I can do it from all that.' (Garry)

> 'Been worth doing.' (Kevin)

> 'Made me feel more positive about myself.' (Shaun)

Asked to give a six-month post-release goal only Dave, being released from his first custodial sentence, cited further education. The others, cautioned by previous resettlement experiences, had lower expectations:

> 'Stay out for six months.' (Garry)

> 'Staying out. Don't know many straight people. It's easier in here.' (Kevin)

> 'To get through my licence without anyone ruining it for me. Good thing is most of my old friends are now in prison.' (Shaun)

However, asked to state a longer-term aim in their lives all four participants cited further education and training related to employment aims:

> 'More IT, graphic design - maybe set up a business.' (Dave)

> 'I want to do anything trade-wise to sort myself out for a few years down the line.' (Garry)

> 'More welding.' (Kevin)

> 'Perhaps more education. Motor mechanics - but that's beyond my reach at the moment.' (Shaun)

These short and long-term ambitions quickly came under pressure as pre-release plans fell apart back in the community, and appeared increasingly unattainable as the weeks progressed. The following accounts give participants' interpretation of events as they negotiated the resettlement process and confronted the reality of life back 'on the out'.

Dave

Background

Age	33
Age at first conviction	31
Custodial sentences	1
School leaving age	15
School qualifications	None
Basic Skills Assessment*	Literacy Level 1
	Numeracy Entry 3
Basic Skills Awards*	Literacy Level 2
	Numeracy Level 2
Other Qualifications*	Start IT
	CLAIT
	Key Skills IT

* Current sentence.

After thirteen months in custody Dave was released from his first prison sentence and returned to live with his partner and her three children. He had little contact with his own two children and said he hadn't lived with his own father after the age of two, but that they were now very close. Dave was proud of his new basic skills accreditation, however he was most enthusiastic about his new IT skills and was keen to develop these on release.

It's broadened my options; I can do database and spreadsheets. It's made everything easier. It was something to do initially, but once I got started I felt I was achieving something. I had to hold myself back to make sure I didn't finish things too quickly. I'm thirty-three and I finally feel I'm achieving something. It's a shame I had to learn it in jail.

Previous work had included catering and taxi driving, and Dave hoped that further IT training would give him the opportunity of employment in an area of interest to him, and possibly self-employment.

Dave had been under mental health care since he was diagnosed with a 'volatile personality disorder' at the age of twenty, and had been on medication and disability benefit since an accident in 2002 which left him with headaches and impaired vision in one eye. Although a 'dope' user for twenty years, Dave felt that alcohol was a bigger problem for him than drugs.

Week 1 – Post Release
Face-to-face interview – Probation Office

One week after release Dave was feeling 'kind of anxious'. 'It's all a bit of a mess at the moment, getting back to normality'. His two main problems were lack of benefit money and adjusting to another change in medication, as it hadn't been possible to maintain continuity of care in prison. 'I take one day's medication and I'm on my back for two days.' 'There should have been more people coming to see me to make sure I had everything I needed on release rather than me having to run from one end of town to the other, making appointments, arranging medication – I'm worn out.' Dave had been referred to a key worker from the Counselling Advice Referral Assessment and Throughcare Service (CARATS), but said he hadn't yet contacted her.

Settling back into the family situation was causing problems for all involved, but Dave was most frustrated at this stage by the fact that having completed a portfolio of work for another IT qualification in prison, his local college had said it would not be possible for him to sit the qualifying test paper without enrolling on the full course; this in spite of intervention by his prison tutor. He felt 'let down and ready to pack it in'.

On a more positive note Dave said he had stayed off alcohol, and asked how his new qualifications might be helping his resettlement he said: 'Without a doubt, definitely. I've found myself sitting down thinking what am I going to do now. I've got ideas, I've got a business I want to set up. Before I wouldn't have thought about that. I feel I can do it if I try hard enough. Having the extra English and maths, plus the IT – it does make a difference because there's no excuse now. I can't sit back and say I'm not qualified.'

Week 2
Face-to-face interview – Probation Office

Dave was still waiting for his first benefit payment and increasingly concerned by the strain this was putting on his situation and relations with his partner: 'I'm going to kick off, which isn't a good thing because I usually get arrested when I do that.' However motivation was renewed with the receipt of his certificates from prison: 'I've been waiting for them for four months, they've finally landed so I can put my portfolio together now. I'll probably do than next week, and my CV … and then I can get focused, because I want to do this. My mum and dad are sort of – let's see if he can, so I want to prove them wrong.' 'Things are a bit more negative than they were. I came out feeling very positive and slowly but surely it's kind of milking away. It's all financial, that's all it is. Once the financial burden's lifted I can focus on other things. With my medication being unbalanced as well it's wearing me out.' But: 'It's going to be okay.'

Weeks 3 - 5
Face-to-face interviews – Probation Office

The following week Dave failed to keep his probation appointment and in week 4 his probation officer reported that Dave had a lot of problems and it would be better for us to meet the next week. In a brief interview during week 5 Dave said 'I didn't think it would be this hard, trying to establish links with family and friends; it's all gone. I knew it would be difficult to begin with, but I wasn't prepared for this.'

Week 6
Face-to-face interview – Probation Office

Dave seemed even more desperate: 'I'm caught in a circle going round and round and round.' 'It's getting harder and harder. I really wish I hadn't come out.' Problems with his partner's fifteen year old daughter had escalated - drugs were involved: 'It's got to the point where it's cheaper to give her the money than it is to replace the stuff she's smashing up.' She had been put on an 'at risk' register following an incident with her mother. 'The authorities aren't helping. We've got social workers coming to our house once a week. We've got child welfare, we've got a community service team, we've got a probation officer – we've got them all coming, but they're no help.' Dave said he missed the settled routine of prison life.

Week 7
Face-to-face interview – Probation Office

Dave was feeling less pressured this week. His benefits had finally been sorted out, his medication seemed to be 'settling down' and the situation at home was more positive: 'It's all coming together'.

Week 11
Face-to-face interview – Dave's home

Visiting Dave at home he talked of continuing problems between himself and his partner due to 'things that were going on when I was in prison'. 'Going to jail ruined my relationship and I'm still trying to rebuild it.' He also reported problems readjusting generally to life outside: 'Going to jail has taken away a lot of my patience. I won't let people push me around. In jail, if someone gives you gyp you slap them round the face, it's as simple as that. That's how you deal with things, I can handle that.'

Inactivity was a growing problem. Dave said he would like to work but had been advised not to until he'd seen a specialist. 'I get bored though, it's my sanity you know and that's what's happening at the moment. Until I find out what the problem is I can't even get a part-time job because I'll end up taking time off sick because of the headaches. Until the scan's done I can't move forward on this.' Dave had missed the original appointment made for a scan and was waiting for another one. He said he'd started drinking quite a lot.

Asked if he had done any more about further IT training Dave said: 'The Tech is only ten minutes away on the bus, half an hour's walk. If I'm truthfully honest with you I think it's all phasing out now. The idea's not as appealing as it was because it's slipping away. I've stepped back into my life and there's so much going on, so much that needs repairing, so much I need to do and it's distracting me. My motivation died when I came home. Even when I came home originally it was like yes, I will do this, I'm going to do this but as time's progressing it doesn't look like it's practical, it doesn't look like it's going to happen. It's not anyone else that's stopping me. A part of it's finance - when you're living off benefit. It's a lifestyle thing. As nice as it sounded, as nice as it probably would be, I don't think it's me.'

Week 15
Face-to-face interview – Dave's home

'I'm drinking a lot more than I should be. I never used to drink you know. It's never been a problem because my dad was a heavy drinker and because of that it kind of always put me off, but stress has been part of it.' Two pit-bull terriers were causing problems, and substantial damage to the house. Dave said he planned to build a kennel for them 'next year.' 'Stephanie (Dave's partner) applied for a job two weeks ago, but we haven't heard anything. She's bored stupid, and where we're spending so much time together we're starting to niggle at each other a little bit, so she's applied for a part time job.' 'If you earn it you're not so keen to spend it. When you're getting your money easily you don't mind spending it, but when you've grafted five days, six days a week for it you're a bit more cautious what you spend it on.'

'Waiting for my scan is becoming a bit – it's a long thing. I can't get on with anything until I know what's going on. I've always worked, but for the last two years I've not been allowed to work and it's slowly, slowly getting the better of me. I'm contemplating starting to decorate just to fill time.'

'We've got quite a lot of issues going on. Stephanie's ex-husband got out today and I'm expecting him to knock at the door. It's a big problem. I bashed his brother when I was in there so he's coming for me. But I spoke to Cliff (Probation Officer) because I was concerned if I hit this guy I'll end up back in jail, so what Cliff's done he's made it part of this guy's licence that he can't come near us, which is a weight off my chest. He has no reason to come here. These are not his children.'

'We're off to Jamaica next year. Her [Stephanie's] dad is signing the hotel and two houses to her so it could proceed into a longer-term thing because I know how to run a hotel.'

Weeks 19-28
Telephone interviews

Over the next few weeks Dave reported that things were just as 'mad' as ever and that 'really nothing's changed'. Stephanie was offered the job she applied for but decided not to take it. 'Money is tight'.

Week 31 – Final Interview
Telephone interview

In his final interview Dave said he felt the most difficult aspect of the last few months had been controlling his anger. He was clearly disappointed that he had abandoned his six-month goal to get another IT qualification: 'I done six months on that course, I done all the course work. I feel really let down.' But he still felt that his improved basic skills gave him more confidence and he didn't rule out further education at some point in the future. He felt 'fairly positive' about staying out of prison and said the thing that would help him most in the immediate future would be getting another date for his brain scan and being able to work. He was no longer in touch with his father.

<u>Garry</u>

Background

Age	21
Age at first conviction	15
Custodial sentences	9
School leaving age	16

School qualifications   "Some"
Basic Skills Assessment   Literacy Entry 3
                                    Numeracy Entry 3
Basic Skills Awards   Literacy Level 1
                                    Numeracy Level 1
Other Qualifications   First Aid
                                    Food Hygiene
                                    Lifting

Prior to his latest custodial sentence Garry lived with his father, his 'best mate'. Like his father, he said, he is an alcoholic. He also cited drug problems, and an inability to control aggressive outbursts. He was not working at the time of his arrest but had worked with his father, a painter and decorator, on a casual basis. He had also had short-term labouring and manufacturing jobs.

Garry was pleased that a place had been found for him at a residential training centre on release, away from the negative influences of his home town: 'You feel this is your last chance.'

Week 1 – Post release
Face-to-face interview – Residential Training Centre

There was a delay on the morning of Garry's release because the terms of his licence stated that he must return to his home town, but a taxi had been sent for him from the residential training centre. However, once installed in his new accommodation Garry said he felt more positive than he had the last time he left prison. His main concern was lack of funds: 'I hate asking for things like fags or borrowing money.'

Garry said he felt the Enhanced Thinking Skills (ETS) course he undertook in prison helped him to deal with the angry outbursts that have repeatedly landed him in trouble. With no alcohol he felt 'more with it', and having allocated jobs to do within the training centre also helped: 'I'm the kind of person I can't just sit about. When I've got a task to do I'm not thinking.' He said Alcoholics Anonymous (AA) contact would be arranged and that basic skills support was available on site, but although Garry found handwriting difficult he said he wasn't ready yet for this. However, he was keen to enrol on a course that would give him a trade skill: 'I want to do anything trade-wise to sort myself out for a few years down the line, because I'm still young.' He planned to be self-employed because 'who wants to have a petty thief, alcoholic, off-his-nut madman working for them.' He was also interested in a money management course because 'I'm useless at money and that.'

Garry was upset that his father hadn't written to him in prison and had failed to turn up for a planned visit. When they met up on his release they argued, but Garry said he respected his father: 'He's overcome such a lot. He doesn't judge me for what I done and that, but the other lot have given up on me because I keeps coming in jail.' Garry appreciated his supportive accommodation: 'This place should help me. I've never had nothing like this before. I've had hostels but they've been bad hostels. Good group of lads here. I feel more positive than any other time I got out of jail.'

Week 2
Face-to-face interview – Residential Training Centre

Garry had not been able to process his benefit claim and had no money. He said he knew how to get it easily enough so it was a challenge resisting the temptation to do so illegally. He was building a good rapport with his key worker to whom he could talk 'instead of bottling it up', and had asked him to arrange an anger management course: 'I need to sort my temper out. When I'm angry I says the first thing that comes into my head.'

Garry was very pleased that he had started and completed two jobs he'd been given during the week: one was moving two piles of grass and the other was domestic. 'That's the first time I've stuck at a job and finished it for three years. I feel good about that – job satisfaction and I've never had that. I done it on my own. On the down side he said he was feeling stressed by some of the other residents: 'One of these days I could just go boom. I'm not saying I'm going to do it, but there's always that possibility.' 'My mind is like a minefield 'cos I gets bad paranoia from when I was doing drugs and that.' Garry did not keep his appointment with AA: 'I don't think I need AA to be honest. I've got more willpower. This is as long as I've been off the beer since I was seventeen.'

'I've been involved in crime since I was a child but it didn't get seriously out of control 'til I was sixteen. I don't see prison as a deterrent.

Prison does my head in, sitting around waiting for lunch and things, you lay on your bed and drift into a half-conscious state, just thinking. Every day I'm out of jail is a bonus. If I can stay out for a year I won't go back to jail – I knows I won't.'

Garry was planning to see his father again: 'My man's like my best mate.' 'Last week I seemed to have more problems than solutions, but this week there seems to be more solutions than problems.'

Week 3
Face-to-face interview – Residential Training Centre

Garry still had no money and his key worker had intervened: 'If my giro turns up today I can sort some stuff out. I'm going to say to my probation officer that if I get my giro today I want to spend the weekend at my old man's. I want to stay out tomorrow night. There's a few people I want to go and see and all that. Not like all the idiots. I'm all right. I had beer chucked at me last night and I said no, I don't want a beer. I'll just stay at my old man's house.' 'I don't want to turn out like him, depending on drink; that's not a life. I don't want to risk getting kicked out of this place just for a couple of beers.'

Garry reported his best week yet at the hostel. He'd done some ground work in a nearby churchyard and some painting and decorating on site. His other reason for feeling buoyant was that he had been to court 'to sort out a couple of issues' and said that he now had a clean slate. He had not yet attended the basic skills classes available at the training centre but was keen to get started on a vocational training: 'That's where all the money is, in the trades.'

'It's one of my top priorities to be working. I know I doss about in this place but that's because you can, but when it comes to working for my life I'll be all right. This place is getting me set up. The training centre is 'like a health farm, not full of down-and-outs and people doing drugs and drink. They've got big hearts in here. You got more support in here than you got in jail or anywhere.' 'When I first hit jail I didn't have nothing. I didn't care about myself, about what I was up to, about anybody or anything whatever. I was down there and it took me about two or three week to get my confidence back, but since I've been here I'm more confident than I've ever been.'

Week 4

The following week Garry was not at the training centre and they didn't know where he was. He had been seen in his home town with some of his old friends and an official recall notice had been put in place. Once located Garry would be sent back to prison to serve the rest of his sentence.

Week 8
Face-to-face interview – HM Prison Winchester

Garry explained: 'I got loads of good mates at home. First visit was okay, but the next time I had money in my pocket. I thought, one beer – but once I starts I can't stop. I kicked-off as soon as the cuffs were off.' He was expecting his new release date to be put back because he'd failed a mandatory prison drug test, but hoped to be out again for his birthday in six weeks. His main concern now was that he might not be able to return to the residential training centre.

Week 13
Face-to-face interview – HM Prison Winchester

After eleven weeks back in prison Garry was once again due for release and had been told that there was a place for him at the training centre for the remaining three months of his licence period, on condition he did not visit his home town. However, he didn't sound very positive: 'If I don't like it I'll just walk out – if someone says something I don't like.' He had once more requested an anger management course, but had rejected suggestions to attend AA: 'My problems are no-one else's business.' Garry said he hoped to stay out of prison for a year this time, but he didn't seem to feel he had much control over the situation: 'I don't know what's happening round the corner – things just happen.'

Week 16
Face-to-face interview – Residential Training Centre

Garry's benefit claim had not yet been processed, but he had received a community grant which he'd spent on clothes and a CD player. He was concerned about possible outstanding criminal charges relating to the period before he was sent back to prison: 'I knew I was going back to jail - I was just enjoying myself for two weeks.' Garry is also sorry to have lost his previous probation officer: 'She showed me respect. She wasn't just bothered about me finishing my licence and that, she was worried about what I'd do in the future, and I've never had that from a probation officer.'

Garry's main concern remained his aggression 'I keeps getting wound up over silly little things. I kicked-off on Monday because I hadn't heard from my old.' 'ETS is the only thing that's helping me outside. It's calmed me down a few times using my thinking skills. From day one I was here and probation's come and see me and I goes, look, I want to set an anger management course up because of my temper, and my temper's the one thing that gets me into trouble. I'm only 22. I could stay out 'til I'm 30 and one day I'll just lose it again. What I wants to do at the moment is get my painting and decorating. I want to get my qualification. I want to set up my own business. I want to go into business with my old man eventually.'

Week 18
Face-to-face interview – Residential Training Centre

Garry said his benefit application had been lost and he had been told to complete more forms. 'I sat there filling them in and I was getting wound up and I thought I ain't doing this. I've gone out, then I walked round the corner and I walked into this shop, and I sees a rack of coats and I thought I could have them straight away. It's money. That's what it boils down to at the moment - money.'

Garry was unhappy that some of his clothes had been stolen off the washing line: 'I know it's petty, but someone nicked my property. If that had happened in prison I'd have jumped on his head. I know I shouldn't speak to you like that, but that's the way I am. I don't like thieves.'

Garry had not been attending his painting and decorating course: 'I can't be bothered with the stress. If I went to this college course this week, I knows I'll end up fighting someone. I'm a volatile person.' 'I work in the kitchen, yeh. I had a knife in my hand. I've looked at it and I had to throw the knife away 'cos I knows if I explode I could have used it. I don't want to end up in jail for years for something like that. I know sometimes

I'm drunk and that and I'm aggressive at the slightest thing and I goes off on one, but there's other times when I just goes off on one anyway, and it's worrying. I want to find out what triggers them off, and control them.

'I don't mind jail, seriously I don't mind it. I got mates in there ... but I don't want to do that no more. It's a waste of time.'

Weeks 21-28

Over the next few weeks Garry returned to his painting and decorating course but then stopped again: 'My head's not on it at the moment. I ain't going to go if I'm stressed out because that's just a problem situation.' He said he had 'messed up' on the test for the first module. He was on an alcohol ban after a heavy drinking session but said he was now attending a drug and alcohol rehabilitation course. He had asked his doctor about the possibility of arranging an anger management course. Although he'd seen his father and arranged to spend Christmas with him, that plan fell through. Garry remained at the training centre and said it was his best New Year ever: 'I got a bit of stability with this place'.

Week 32 – Final Interview
Face-to-face interview – Residential Training Centre

At his final interview Garry said he'd decided to remain at the training centre even though his licence period was over: 'It's kept me under control.' 'This is the longest I been out of jail. I ain't got no up and coming things or nothing.' He said a job was the thing that would most improve his current circumstances and that his key worker was helping him to look for labouring or manufacturing work outside the training centre. He had received a letter from his doctor to say that there were no anger management courses available in the area.

Kevin

Background
Age   24
Age at first conviction   16
Custodial sentences   "lots"
School leaving age   "13 or 14"
School qualifications   None

Basic Skills Assessment	Literacy Entry 3
	Numeracy Level 1
Basic Skills Awards	Literacy Level 1
Other Qualifications	Welding
	NVQ Level 1 Engineering
	Carpentry

Kevin said his father died of a drug overdose when he was seven and he lived with his grandmother until the age of ten when, as 'a little terrorist', he was taken into care. Since then he has rarely lived outside an institution, progressing from young offender institutions to prison. Prior to his current custodial sentence he was living with his girlfriend, and their baby daughter. Although he has 'qualifications coming out of my ears' he has had little work experience outside prison. Kevin was assessed as 'hyperactive' in his youth and said cannabis controlled his behaviour better than his prescribed medication.

Kevin applied for prison education 'to pass the time' and said he felt more positive about employment as a result of improved basic skills because, he said, the numeracy helped with the welding he wants to pursue, and he could now write a CV. He also felt that his certificates would help. Although his previous attempts at resettlement had failed, he felt his responsibilities as a father would give him greater motivation.

Week 1 – Post Release

Kevin returned to his girlfriend's home on release to find that she was now engaged to someone else; a friend of his.

Week 2
Telephone interview

Kevin said he was feeling 'elated' at being out of prison after three years but felt 'seriously battered' by the situation with his girlfriend, and lack of access to his daughter. He was staying with an aunt but this was 'difficult'. He hadn't applied for benefits because, on the strength of his carpentry skills, he'd got a job making pallets.

Week 3

Probation Office: Kevin didn't keep his appointment.

Week 4
Telephone interview

Lack of stable accommodation had been Kevin's biggest problem since release and he was 'dossing with friends' at this point. He was still working and felt that having a job was the thing that would keep him out of prison. He said he wasn't able to give any thought to further education or training in his current situation. The police wanted to talk to him about outstanding issues.

Week 5
Telephone interview

Probation had found Kevin a hostel place and he sounded positive: 'Well, I've got somewhere to live now, and a job, haven't I.'

Week 6
Face-to-face interview – A pub

Kevin had been evicted from the hostel for smoking cannabis and was staying with his aunt again. He was very happy about a young girl he'd met at the hostel who was 'the best thing that's happened to me.' He was also positive about the pallet construction job which he had on a six-month trial basis. 'The carpentry course gave me a foot in the door. I do like getting up and going to work with others, and other people know you're going to work. It feels good. It keeps you in a routine. Out here I'm working for life, inside I'm just working for extra burn [tobacco]. I never thought I could feel so determined.'

Week 8
Face-to-face interview – Probation Office

Kevin had been told he might get laid off work: 'Last in, first out.' He was looking for other work: 'I looked around a few agencies when I first got out, but none of them were taking anyone on. If you've got a criminal record a lot of them won't take you. I've lost all my certificates anyway; my engineering ones, my welding - everything, my maths, the English.'

Accommodation with his aunt was uncertain: 'It isn't easy for either of us.' His relationship with his new girlfriend was strained because, he said, he couldn't cope with her problems.

'Seriously, I'm thinking about going back [to prison]. I'm having too much shit thrown at me. I get and I'm trying to sort my life out, things start going well and then they just collapse. I can't do it again. You've got the boys to moan at in jail, and you can have employment. It don't matter if you've got a criminal record in jail, you get a job anyway. I was happy where I was. I feel so old. I've come out of jail six times and every time it happens the same, every time. Why every time, why? If I get laid off on Friday where am I going to come up with £200? (for accommodation deposit). 'I'll find someone else to focus on. When it's just about me I don't give a f... I'll happily go out, do the crime, go to jail, go out, do the crime, go to jail. If I've got someone else to focus on - I've got my daughter but I don't see her a lot.

Week 10
Telephone interview

Kevin rang to cancel our meeting because he had to go to the benefit office. He had applied for sheet metal work through the Job Centre, but meanwhile was 'out on the earn'.

Week 11
Telephone inverview

Kevin had received a letter of rejection for the sheet metal work so was completing more job applications and trying building sites for casual work. He was staying with various friends and his aunt.

Week 12
Face-to-face interview – Sitting on a wall in town

Kevin was now staying a couple of nights a week with the mother of his daughter, who was no longer engaged to his friend. This was giving him time with his daughter and, he said, it meant he could do his washing. He was now receiving benefit money and had stopped looking for work: 'I'm concentrating on being a father at the moment.'

Week 16
Telephone interview

Kevin's new arrangement with his ex-girlfriend had gone 'pear-shaped'. He said a solicitor was arranging access to his daughter and he was again living with his aunt. He had no job but was hoping to get some refurbishment work through a friend.

Week 23
Face-to-face interview – Home of a new girlfriend

Kevin had now reached the end of his licence period and was living with a new girlfriend, his elder by some years, and her three children. He said he had stopped claiming benefit, was still job hunting but was meanwhile 'hustling'; buying things and selling them on. 'One thing I am doing is avoiding trouble.' He said he wanted to apply for welding work at the docks but that this was 'dodgy' because it involved drug testing, 'so my weekends would be straight out the window.'

Week 33 – Final Interview
Face-to-face interview – Home of new girlfriend

Kevin still had no job and felt his criminal record was a key issue. He said he still wanted to develop his welding skills and had applied for a welding job at the docks. He was clearing his system in anticipation of a drug test.

Kevin was pleased to have achieved his six-month goal to stay out of prison and said his new girlfriend was the most positive thing that had happened since his release. Losing his pallet job was the most negative: 'Never once while I was working did I think about going out and doing stupid stuff.' He said he felt 'fairly positive about staying out of prison' and that a job would represent the biggest improvement in his immediate circumstances, with further welding qualifications still a longer-term aim.

<u>Shaun</u>

Background	
Age	28
Age at first conviction	15
Custodial sentences	3
School leaving age	14
School qualifications	None
Basic Skills Assessment	Literacy Entry 3
	Numeracy Entry 2
Basic Skills Awards	Literacy Entry 3
	Numeracy Level 2
Other Qualifications	Bricklaying
	Painting & Decorating

Shaun was living with his mother prior to his current sentence and had worked for ten years laying playground safety surfaces. Although his father left home when Shaun was three, they had maintained contact and Shaun described his father as his 'best mate'.

Shaun was assessed as dyslexic at his secondary school and attended a special school until he left at fourteen. He attributes his criminal record to drug addiction and said he wished he could 'go back ... to the beginning of my life when things started to go pear-shaped, and then take the other route and be a normal person and not take drugs and that.' 'I've got to the stage in my life when I don't want to come back to prison' but 'I was determined last time.'

Shaun said he applied for prison education because 'I want to get better in my own mind. I want to get to the stage where I don't have to ask my mum to fill in a job application.' Although he felt frustrated by having to repeat work each time he returned to prison, he said the basic skills support he received helped with the written element of the reasoning and rehabilitation course he did and 'made me feel more positive about myself.' 'I can send text messages on the phone.' Shaun said that when he left prison last time, with improved basic skills, he felt 'top of the ladder, then knocked back down.'

Week 1 – Post release
Telephone interview

Shaun said his Job Seekers Allowance was being processed and that he had an appointment with New Deal the following week, as well as one with Options, the drug and alcohol counselling service. He wasn't working and said he'd be willing to accept almost any job, but felt his criminal record would be a big problem. Things were fine back home with his mother, but he felt 'pressured' by appointments.

Week 3
Face-to-face interview – Probation Office

Shaun felt more relaxed this week and was relieved that an outstanding case had been dismissed in court on Monday. However, he said he'd be in court again next month on a 'handling' charge. He said his improved literacy skills were helping with job applications but also that he would prefer to find work through friends as he felt insecure in a new environment. 'People keep harassing me to get work and that, you know what I mean. This is what does my head in more than anything else. Independent, that's what I want to be and people seem to be not letting me and keep butting into my life when all I want to do is get on with things and be independent.'

Shaun had a key worker and was now receiving drug and alcohol counselling: 'I've managed to keep it under control at the moment. I've got everything in place to help me and that, it's just, I don't know, it's hard for me to explain. There's loads of things going round in my head all the time. Once I've got properly settled down and that - like I say, I've only been out three and a half weeks. Shaun said he hadn't seen his father since his release and didn't know where he was.

Week 7
Telephone interview

Things were still 'hectic, a bit mad, but that's my lifestyle. It'll settle down when I've got a job and everything.' Having missed some of his drug rehabilitation sessions he was on a waiting list to start again. He was relieved that he'd been given another six month's probation for his outstanding charges instead of the anticipated custodial sentence: 'Now I can look ahead.' Shaun hadn't been able to get the work he'd hoped for through friends, but was pleased that Jobcentre Plus had offered him a forklift truck course.

Week 8
Telephone interview

Shaun was unhappy because Jobcentre Plus had said they would not accept the 'Preparation for Work' certificate he gained in prison and that he'd have to do the course again before they could allow him to do the forklift truck training. HMP Winchester Job Club said they would look into the matter. Shaun said things were all right at home and that he was attending Options again for his drug addition.

Week 9
Face-to-face interview – Probation Office

There was an incident at home this week involving the police: with his mother away Shaun had given refuge to a friend wanted by the police, which may cause him problems. However his main concern was that Jobcentre Plus had confirmed they wouldn't accept the OCN Preparation for Work certificate he gained in prison, in spite of intervention by the prison Job Club. Jobcentre Plus said the forklift truck course providers wouldn't accept it, but the course providers said it was a decision for Jobcentre Plus. Shaun said he was not prepared to repeat the course. He'd been asking around for work: 'It's whether it comes along or not. I've put the wheels in motion, it's up to people to get back to me. You just don't know what's round the corner - anything can happen.' But, 'I'll get there.'

Week 14
Shaun's home

He was not there at the agreed interview time.

Week 19
Telephone interview

Shaun was pleased that he'd heard no more from the police. He was still not working but was attending his Options rehabilitation sessions and felt more positive.

Week 26 – Final Interview
Telephone interview

Shaun had been difficult to contact and said he didn't have time for a final face-to-face interview. However, he was willing to talk briefly on the 'phone and said he was very pleased to be back at his old job of laying playground surfaces. He'd given up on his rehabilitation course and said he had things under control himself: 'I stay in most evenings.' Having realised his six-month goal to stay out of prison he felt very confident about his ability to remain out in the future. Although he had expressed an interest in further education or training prior to his release his main concern now was to keep his job. He felt that getting his old job back was the most positive thing to have happened since his release, and not being able to do the forklift truck course the most negative.

'It's a lifestyle thing'

The four participants of this study returned to different situations on release and faced a complex combination of issues in their efforts to re/settle into the community, but against the turbulent backdrop of their lives none of their further education or training aspirations were able to maintain a foothold. The range and extent of resettlement problems experienced by the participants suggest the need for pre-release assessment, planning and provision on an individual basis, but the factor common to them all was the limited practical and inner resources they had to tackle their problems, and to re-order their lives in such a way that would enable them to progress and to improve their situations.

The ability to exploit or develop improved basic skills and other qualifications gained through prison education has to be assessed in the wider context of resettlement. The barriers to resettlement faced by the participants: access to benefits, employment, accommodation, personal relationships, pending criminal proceedings, mental and physical health problems as well as substance misuse, all demonstrate the need for a comprehensive and effective programme of support to help those leaving prison to re/establish a viable position in the community. Of the four participants only Dave had ever sustained a fully independent adult life in the community prior to custody. While balancing the need to support against the danger of 'learned helplessness' (HM Inspectorates of Prisons and Probation, 2001), it is clear that for someone like Garry intensive and long-term support are essential to break the cycle of re-offending. It is to be hoped that the establishment of NOMS, the amalgamation of the Prison and Probation Services into a National Offender Management Service, will help to bridge the gulf between the emasculated world of prison life and harsh reality of life back in the mainstream, and prevent ex-prisoners from 'falling in the gap between two different services' (Blunkett, 2004). Similarly the new Offenders' Learning and Skills Service (OLASS), 'aimed at better integrating learning and skills provision in both custody and the community' (Forum on Prisoner Education, 2005), will hopefully effect a similar co-ordination of resources, but for the participants of this study the lack of attention given to continuing education or training support on release meant that much was lost both in terms of learning and morale. Established patterns of employment and further education and training need to be developed through day-release into the local community prior to release, and the necessary support given to those 'making the cultural leap ... converting the new confidence into a concrete objective' (Probation Officer).

That improved basic skills *per se* are not sufficient to bring about lasting change is supported by the first longitudinal study of basic skills training for prisoners to be undertaken in England and Wales. In a two year study of over four hundred and fifty offenders, the Home Office's Research, Development and Statistics Directorate (RDS) concluded that 'improving prisoners' basic skills alone is unlikely to have a major impact on their prospects for successful resettlement' (Stewart, 2005). While 'half of all prisoners are at or below level 1 (the level expected on an 11-year-old) in reading; two-thirds in numeracy; and four-fifths in writing' (Social Exclusion Unit, 2002) the need for basic skills education in prisons is not in doubt, but 'while a lack of basic skills may debar people from 96 per cent of jobs, a knowledge of basis skills alone is not a qualification for many more' (Uden, 2004).

The RDS research, like that of the present study, focused on prisoners who were assessed at or below level I in literacy or numeracy, but in 'the world's first large-scale, comparative assessment of adult literacy' the Organisation for Economic Co-operation and Development (OECD) led an international study looking at literacy from levels I to 5. This found significant employment and educational benefits for those with literacy skills at level 3 or above, level 3 being 'considered by experts as a suitable minimum skill level for coping with the demands of modern life and work'. The study acknowledged that up to three-quarters of adults fail to attain this level of literacy and stated that the 'challenge facing all countries is how to overcome the disparity between the rising demand for skills in the knowledge economy and the presence in the workforce of large numbers of people with poor literacy skills'. It also found that 'formal educational attainment is the main determinant of literacy proficiency', but 67% of the RDS research sample left school before the age of 16, as did three of the four participants of this study, (OECD, 2000).

It requires a considerable investment of time and effort on the part of the adult learner to make significant and sustained improvements in basic skills and to progress to higher levels, and there is no simple answer to engaging those most in need. A study initiated by the National Institute of Adult Continuing Education (NIACE) into 'men who are missing from education and training', found that men who left school before sixteen with no qualifications, and who fell into the skilled or unskilled manual occupations groups, were least likely to take advantage of new access to learning initiatives (McGivney, 1999), and a later NIACE study found that the few who qualify beyond level 2 in prison return mainly to unskilled work on release (Uden, 2004). Although the four participants of this study chose to enrol on prison education, three did so initially to pass the time in a restricted and regulated environment with few attractive alternatives, and given their circumstances on release it isn't surprising that none successfully pursued further learning opportunities. As Dave and Shaun demonstrated, the first hurdle is enough to undermine confidence and motivation, and for those 'from low income families, finding work is a greater priority than gaining qualifications' (McGivney, 1999).

While basic skills are the essential first step out of low-skilled, low wage employment, there is a need to encourage those motivated to improve their lives to develop a long-term approach to learning, integrated into work-related activities, that will take them beyond basic skills and give them access to continuing personal development.

> ... the workplace is a factor in literacy acquisition and maintenance, a place where a considerable amount of reading, writing and arithmetic takes place. Often these two aspects of workplace literacy reinforce each other: skills learned in schools facilitate engaging more frequently in more complex activities at the workplace that in turn build skills. (OECD, 2000)

While 'the prison service has invested £4.5 million over the past two years in upgrading vocational training workshops across the prison estate' (House of Commons Home Affairs Committee, 2005), the ONS study reported that 80% of their prison sample received basic skills training delivered in a classroom setting (Stewart, 2005), as did the four participants of this study. This is a missed opportunity, especially for those in prison who have never developed a sustained work ethic. 'Prison work should strive to supply the same range of incentives and benefits which make legitimate work in the community worthwhile: namely job satisfaction, disposable income, self-esteem, personal development, social integration, social status, and the ability to plan and save for the future' (www.howardleague.org 2000 cited by HM Inspectorates of Prisons and Probation, 2001). In their final interviews all four participants cited employment as the crucial factor in changing their lives.

Disclosure

The value of any accreditation gained through prison education and training is greatly diminished when attached to a criminal record. The £122 million of additional investment for 2004-05 to support learning and skills provision in prisons (House of Commons Home Affairs Committee, 2005) is recognition of the significant role of employment in resettlement, and the reduction of re-offending rates. But there seems to be a contradiction in the efforts of Government to help offenders into work and the establishment of the Criminal Records Bureau, following the Police Act 1997, which is likely to make it more difficult for those with a criminal record to obtain legitimate employment in the future.

This agency currently provides details of those applying for 'sensitive' employment only, but when fully operational it is proposed that any employer will be able to ask an applicant to apply through the Criminal Records Bureau for a Criminal Conviction Certificate, which will carry details of all unspent convictions. Under the Rehabilitation of Offenders Act 1974 (ROA), a sentence of more than two and a half years can never be considered 'spent', burdening many ex-offenders with a criminal record for life.

It is estimated that only about 4% of crimes against individuals and their property result in a conviction or caution, meaning that many job applicants have committed crimes but do not have a criminal record (Trades Union Congress – ESAD, 2001). It seems unjust therefore that those who have been convicted of crimes attracting moderate sentences, and have served their time, should be doubly penalised by the stigma of a criminal record many years after re-integration into the community.

'Over a quarter of the working age population has a previous conviction … but a criminal record can seriously diminish employment opportunities' (www.homeoffice.gov.uk/justice 22/04/2004). The Gardiner Committee, reporting back in 1972, stated that 'the general aim of rehabilitation laws should be to restore the offender to a position in society not less favourable than that of one who has not offended' (Justice et al, 1972), and in a more recent consultation paper to Ministers reviewing the ROA it was recommended 'that the disclosure period should comprise the period of the sentence plus an additional buffer zone' (Home Office, 2002). As yet there is no timetable to implement such recommendations.

Social inclusion has been a key theme in New Labour policy since it came to power in 1997, when Prime Minister Blair promised to 'build a nation united, with common purpose, shared values, with no-one shut out or excluded' (Levitas, 1998), and the Social Exclusion Unit, set up in 1997 to provide 'innovative thinking in addressing some of society's most difficult problems' (www.socialexclusion.gov.uk 03/05/2005), was an early response to this imperative.

By falling outside the law offenders are 'not seen as qualifying for full citizenship' and 'the sense of lesser eligibility may continue after the punishment has ended, through the socially and economically disabling effect of criminal conviction' (Faulkner, 2001). Ex-offenders, those who have served the sentence deemed appropriate by society for their crimes, and who have successfully completed a probationary period back in the community, would be better placed to embrace the responsibilities of citizenship without the stigma of an enduring criminal record.

More large-scale research over a longer period is needed to gain a better understanding of the link between prison education and reduced rates of re-offending, but this small study suggests that those returning to the community with new basic skills accreditation need a green light policy if they are to build on their achievements, re/enter the labour market and access the opportunites for continuing development that will benefit both them and society.

Bibliography

Blunkett, D (2004); Reducing Crime - Changing Lives. London: Home Office

Faulkner, D (2001); Crime, State and Citizen: A Field Full of Folk. Winchester: Waterside Press

HM Inspectorate of Prisons (2001); Through the Prison Gate: A Joint Thematic Review by HM Inspectorates of Prisons and Probation. London: Home Office.

Home Office (2002); Breaking the Circle - A Report of the Review of the Rehabilitation of Offenders Act, London: Home Office Communication Directorate

House of Commons (2005); Seventh Report from the Education and Skills Committee: Prison Education: Session 2004 – 2005. Volume I (HC114-11). London: The Stationery Office.

House of Commons (2005); Rehabilitation of Prisoners: first report of session 2004-05 Volume I. London: The Stationery Office.

Justice, the Howard League for Penal Reform and the National Association for the Care and Resettlement of Offenders (1972); Living It Down - The Problem of Old Convictions. London: Stevens & Sons

Levitas, R (1998); The Inclusive Society? Social Exclusion and New Labour. Basingstoke: Palgrave

McGivney, V (1999); Excluded Men - Men who are Missing from Education and Training. Leicester: NIACE

Organisation for Economic Co-operation and Development (OECD) (2000); Literacy in the Information Age. Paris: OECD

Social Exclusion Unit (2002); Reducing Reoffending by Ex-Prisoners. London: Social Exclusion Unit

Stewart, D (2005) An Evaluation of Basic Skills Training for Prisons (The Research, Development and Statistics Directorate, Home Office Findings 260), London: Home Office

Taylor, S (2005); Forum News - Issue 6. London: Forum on Prisoner Education

Trades Union Congress (TUC), Economic and Social Affairs Department (2001); Employment and Ex-offenders. London: TUC

Uden, T (2004); Learning's Not A Crime. Leicester: NIACE

Higher Barriers:
Ex-Prisoners and University Admissions

Daniel Hayward

Introduction

"Increasing university attendance to 50 per-cent of those under thirty by 2010 is a government priority" (Quinn et al, 2005). Thomas (2000) points out that we are increasing access to higher education and widening participation among the non-traditional groups. Perhaps we have lessons to learn from our industrialised competitors. Could it be that some of the potential entrants to universities, the 'non-traditional students' are being overlooked? Recent research notes, "Higher Education in the UK has been falling behind industrialised competitors in funding increases and student entry rates, according to new figures from Organisation of Economic Co-operation and Development (OECD)" (NIACE, 2005: p. 5).

The aim of this research was to gather the views of universities, students and the various bodies concerned with higher education and the admissions processes for applicants. Primary data was drawn from universities in the United Kingdom and to introduce a comparative element, European universities were also contacted. *Breaking the Circle* notes that approximately 6% of individuals leaving prison reported having an education or training place to go to (Home Office, 2002). The most recent government report notes that 40,000 offenders leaving prison in 2004/2005 declared that they had an education, training or employment place on release (Home Office, 2005). Why, then, does the majority of research find reconviction rates in England & Wales ranging from 50% to 80%, depending on a number of other variables such as age, ethnicity and gender (Home Office, 2003)?

Education slows the revolving door of incarceration and reincarceration. Research in Canada, North America and England, illustrates the value of participation in education, not only does it reduce offending behaviour and incidents of crime; the investment in education on the part of society is far outweighed by the economic savings to society. The win-win is an active and productive individual who does not commit crime. The most important factors when looking at the effect of education on reducing levels of recidivism are: longevity of educational journey; the continuity of provision, whether from community to custody, at points of transfer in custody or from custody to community and; the individual focus of education - treating students as subjects, not objects (Freire, 1996; Duguid, 1998; Pawson, 2000; Harper & Chitty 2005).

An opportunity for change?

The increased focus of the Government and the Department for Education & Skills (DfES) and the more recent involvement of the Learning & Skills Council (LSC) in offender education, welcome as it may be, still effectively disadvantages those students wishing to pursue academic study at higher levels; the focus of key performance targets/indicators is premised on the nostrum of increasing basic skills accreditations. The attainment of such accreditations is often proclaimed as a panacea that will ultimately lead to a reduction in offending via education through, or coupled with, employment; for many the reality is different. Home Office Research Study 291 published some time after the governmental drive to increase basic skills, not surprisingly found research supporting the argument that basic skills training contributed to a reduction in re-offending; the omission of research into those students who study higher education in the United Kingdom and the effect this may have on re-offending patterns is an area that must be addressed (Harper & Chitty 2005).

The House of Commons Education & Skills Committee were concerned that existing prison education policy, skewed towards basic skills provision, has been based on a hunch. The Committee wished, "the Government to undertake thorough and robust research to identify what type of education and training provision will have the greatest impact on meeting the individual needs of the prisoner and providing them with real alternatives to crime on release" (House of Commons, 2005). Distance learning provision in prisons provides one avenue for education at higher levels although this is largely under-resourced and far too reliant on the work of the Prisoners' Education Trust. There is a worry that a lack of access to the internet by prisoners may severely restrict the role of the Open University, increasingly moving to delivery of courses through the internet, in prison education; another door slams shut.

Research by Hamlyn & Lewis (2000), which looked into the prior educational attainment of female prisoners, found that 37% had participated in further education and 4% had attended higher education. Similarly, Irish research found that just over 15% of adult prisoners had ability needs at levels four and five, well beyond basic skills level (Morgan & Kett 2003). Research has indicated that in one category 'D' prison in England 69% of prisoners had achieved GSCE "O" Level grades or above prior to imprisonment; 29% had A-levels and 31% had degree and/or postgraduate qualifications (Ingleby, 2005).

The stark reality is that at a national level we do not know the true capability of our prisoners. Accurate assessment of needs and automated capture, storage and analysis of individual data is woefully lacking in the present system. We are promised that the National Offender Management Service (NOMS) and C-NOMIS, the new Service's computer software system, will deliver a ten per-cent reduction in reoffending. To date, this far from seamless service is anticipated to be fully operational by 2009 (Home Office, 2005). There is a clear and urgent need for this effective management information system that can be accessed by all those agencies, voluntary and statutory that can aid an individuals' pursuit of education, subject to the limitations of the Data Protection Act and with individual consent to information sharing. At present, poor information, advice and guidance, prohibits a continuous learning journey. The heralded seamless educational provision from community to custody, custody to community and in some cases back once more to custody is still a vision, not a reality; it is still the holy grail for government, prisoners, staff and our society. The rationale underpinning the service places the emphasis very much on the word individual; the individual offender manager and individual responsibility.

The blueprint for changes to the delivery of offender education for adult prisoners is found in, the *Offenders' Learning Journey*. Section 1:5 states, "that offenders, in prison and supervised in the community, according to need, should have access to learning and skills which enables them to gain the skills and qualifications they need to hold down a job and have a positive role in society". The emphasis on enabling offenders to gain skills and qualifications appears admirable, yet unless societal attitudes are changed and criminal pasts not continually re-visited then the words will be little more than intentions and aspirations. Universities could be encouraged to recruit applicants with criminal convictions. A huge threat that society faces stems from the growing social and economic costs of continual exclusion. We must move away from the assumption that past behaviour does in fact predict future action; individuals must be given a second chance. First, research tells us that between a quarter and a half of all young men are active criminals prior to the age of eighteen (Lam & Harcourt, 2003). Second, we know the majority of men desist from crime in their late twenties and early thirties (Kanzawa & Still, 2000). Third, ex-prisoners and ex-offenders face stigma and discrimination on the basis of their past (Fletcher et al, 2001).

It is true to say that we live in a 'risk society', where labels such as, offender, prisoner, criminal, deviant, (and to these the prefixes 'former' and 'ex-' could be added) can and do lead to discrimination and stigma in various guises and in differing situational contexts: the stereotypes associated when such labels are conferred on individuals are unhelpful to any process of rehabilitation, and at times patently erroneous. Rehabilitation and resettlement for many is a fallacy as such notions presuppose a level of success in these areas prior to punishment. This is often not the case (Farrall & Sparks, 2006). In instances where the Criminal Records Bureau (CRB) is used to provide information for disclosure checks, the discrimination can be exacerbated by 'other relevant information'. Often the inclusion of such information remains untested and unproven in a court of law. For the purpose of this research I will be using the term criminal conviction which refers to those who declare that they have criminal convictions, or are revealed to have such convictions. However that information arises, it is they that potentially face the greatest discrimination.

For the benefit of society, the rule of law and, where they exist, mechanisms for punishment must provide genuine hope – not empty words – for those who wish to change. We must not be driven by a primordial passion for revenge. Those who participate in education and training are three times less likely to be re-convicted (Social Exclusion

Unit, 2002). As a society, what have we to lose? At present an investment in education for offenders under supervision, prisoners, ex-prisoners and ex-offenders must be a priority in order that the cycle of criminality is broken for even a few. Society must not scupper gains made in prison, in the limited cases that it performs a rehabilitative function, because of discriminatory practices on release into the community; we must not fail in our task to provide adequate education and training opportunities for those under supervision in the community.

As a caveat, there are many factors in addition to education and training that influence the propensity to offend and subsequently re-offend, to disaggregate the variables is not without problems. Home Office (2004) identified a number of strands that must be tackled in order to reduce re-offending, although the current NOMS national and regional action plans need supporting by legislative change. One problem that students face when they wish to continue their education, as for that matter do potential employees, is the requirement in certain cases to disclose past convictions. If we consider that students with criminal convictions may have problems with housing, debt and perhaps mental health problems then society should be more accommodating and not less. The most severe sanction that the United Kingdom has is prison; we imprison better than any other country in Western Europe. Let us hope that our fervent attitude to punish, and hold accountable for crimes committed, can be tempered by a willingness to genuinely ensure that those who wish to make a new life have the fullest support of the State.

A Canadian educational research project, with a cohort of 654, investigated whether participation in education by prisoners and ex-prisoners led to a reduced likelihood of re-offending. Using a previously designed recidivism prediction score as a benchmark for comparison, the large cohort was split into sub-groups. Significantly, in a majority of cases those who participated in education were likely to re-offend less frequently on release, than the recidivism prediction score would have indicated. One of the most dramatic results was that the two hundred and thirteen individuals who continued with education after release out performed the recidivism prediction score by 45% (Duguid, 1998).

Criminal convictions and disclosure

Individuals who have been found guilty or pleaded guilty to a criminal offence are by definition the criminally convicted. This does not necessarily imply those labelled are guilty of a criminal act, nor does the lack of such a label mean that an individual has not committed a criminal act. Literally taken, the word disclosure means a process of revealing information; in the context of this research the term disclosure is taken as a societal mechanism to compel individuals who have been labelled the 'criminally convicted' to make others aware, in certain circumstances, of this fact. In the United Kingdom, the lengthy rehabilitation periods contained in legislation known as the Rehabilitation of Offenders Act (ROA) 1974, which governs the requirement for individuals to 'disclose', do not allow, in a growing number of cases, the past to be forgotten when an individual seeks employment or education; individuals are free from prison but not from stigmatisation.

In trying to reduce re-offending, crime and ultimately in pursuit of a safer society where former offenders become citizens who are more responsible, take responsibility and are given support to play a greater role in the wider community, we face a problem. It is difficult to reconcile arguments that offenders should have more positive rights such as entitlement to help and support following their offending. It is clear the media has a greater role to play in ensuring that the public are informed as to the merits of trying to find a solution to this perennial problem.

Arguments against protecting or giving ex-offenders' rights are often rooted in property rights arguments stating that the owners of the property should be able to do what they wish with that property; educators and employers have discretion unless legislation or incentives under the market mechanism determines otherwise. Property rights are not sacrosanct and the Government could intervene to ensure that rights were more balanced to benefit the greater good not the status quo. Compulsory purchase of land for a highways project provides an example of such an intervention. In the case of higher education it is imperative that individuals with criminal convictions are encouraged into universities where society could benefit from their higher education.

The Gardiner Committee 1972

The Gardiner Committee of 1972 recognised the difficulties that an ex-offender faced when attempting to resettle into the community because of the growing use by employers of criminal conviction information. At the time, when societal attitudes believed 'a job was for life' and 'university education was not for the working classes', securing employment following a custodial sentence was seen as one of the main ways that effective resettlement could be ensured. However, the desired situation was often thwarted because of an individual's criminal past. The aim of the Gardiner Committee was to restore somebody back into society, when released from prison, in a position that is no less favourable than one who has not offended; that aspiration is still far from reality.

The ROA 1974, borne out of the recommendations of the Gardiner Committee, was designed to regulate offenders and ex-offenders. Although it did not fulfil the aspirations of the Gardiner Committee, it did provide codified rules on rehabilitation periods – the length of rehabilitation still depends on the length of sentence and not the offence committed - and enabled some criminal convictions to become spent (ignored after a certain rehabilitation period). Age at the time of offence has a bearing on rehabilitation periods. The exceptions to this are:

- Sentences over 30 months never become spent;
- Sentences under 30 months can become spent and there is a sliding scale based on the initial sentence length;
- Disclosure periods are effectively compounded by multiple offences;
- Exceptions have been introduced for certain employment positions ostensibly in order to protect the public and mainly for posts working with children and the vulnerable. In such cases organisations are entitled to take into account all previous convictions both spent and unspent when assessing the suitability of an individual (Nacro, 2002).

For individuals falling into the above categories the ROA 1974 makes it quite clear that the onus is on the individual to disclose this information to any organisation that asks, subject to the provisions of the ROA 1974, and in certain circumstances the exceptions order of 1975. If an individual fails to disclose 'relevant' unspent information or spent information, when asked to do so it is possible that prosecution may follow. The ROA 1974 allows any organisation, universities and colleges included, to ask for details of unspent convictions but provides a level of protection for those people whose convictions are deemed 'spent' under the act, save for access to specific courses. The ROA 1974 is not concerned with attempting to rehabilitate those who do not wish to be rehabilitated.

In July 2002 a review of the ROA 1974, *Breaking the Circle*, was completed. The main findings of the review were:

- The objectives of the ROA 1974 are valid yet it does not achieve an adequate balance between resettlement and protection;
- The act is confusing, offenders and organisations know very little about the provisions contained in the ROA 1974;
- 'Sentence inflation' has widened the net of those whose convictions will never be spent; a growing number of individuals being sentenced to custody over 30 months;
- ROA 1974 criticised for disadvantaging individuals who cease to pose a danger to the public;
- Educational establishments, like employers, can require disclosure. The review of the ROA 1974 focused on the impact of the requirement to disclose on employment prospects not on educational opportunities (Home Office, 2002).

With nearing 30,000 prisoners serving sentences over four years in any given year, perhaps half the prison population at any given time will have sentences that never become spent (Prison Reform Trust, 2005). The numbers of individuals sentenced to prison terms has risen inexorably and exponentially in the last thirty years. In 1972 when the Gardiner Committee sat there were under 40,000 prisoners in the system, we are now just shy of 80,000 (Home Office, 2002). Regional variations in sentencing patterns impact on individuals and groups. Conviction bias, severity of sentencing and the larger use of remand for women and black and minority ethnic groups means that the ROA 1974 disproportionately impacts on them; briefing papers issued by the Prison Reform Trust in 2005 reveal this pattern.

Fairness and transparency of higher education - how about access?

"A number of students also expressed interest in attending university after their release, a few were in the process of making enquiries or completing applications at the time of interview. Sean, whilst still interested in photography, was hoping to earn a degree in sports studies or psychology at university. He had applied to five universities. The two he had already heard back from advised him to reapply after he had been out of prison for twelve months. He was still waiting to hear from the others" (Hughes, 2004: p. 53).

Whilst the Schwartz Review did catalogue obstacles for some groups applying for places at universities it failed to do more than superficially touch, with a fleeting reference to CRB, upon the problems that those applicants, with criminal convictions – 'spent' or 'unspent', can face when applying to university. The autonomy that universities wield is reflected in the numerous admissions procedures. Whilst the recommendations contained in Schwartz have opened up the debate in this area and the consultation headed by Sir Alan Wilson, Director General at the Higher Education Directorate at the Department for Education and Skills (DfES) may offer further insights, in all the literature surrounding fair admissions there is little to suggest that stigma and potential discrimination, faced by a sizeable and growing minority of those who declare they have a criminal conviction, will be addressed (DFES, 2004).

Setting aside the provisions contained in the outdated ROA 1974 which preclude admission onto a minority of courses and effectively make the process more difficult, there seem to be no comprehensive guidelines for universities to make informed, transparent, and fair decisions based on conviction information that they may receive. At present UCAS, the DfES and the CRB amongst a line of others, all well placed to offer such guidance, seem reluctant to shoulder the responsibility. There are over three hundred prisoner-students who register annually for Open University courses (Taylor, 2005). As the DfES notes, "Support for offenders taking higher education has increased significantly in recent years: the number of undergraduate opportunities rose from 450 in 2002-03 to 1,050 in 2005-06, in addition to 250 access courses" (DfES, 2005: p. 16). The Prisoners' Education Trust receives funds through the Offenders' Learning & Skills Unit (OLSU), enabling it to provide fees for courses, although only two thirds of applicants requiring funding receive it such is the shortfall in total funds.

It is clear that we do not know the true numbers of those with criminal convictions wishing to access university education; that data is not collated centrally is a travesty, for if we do not have facts at our disposal we cannot begin to understand what resources, and more importantly the way to allocate such resources, are needed. Potentially, all Open University prisoner-students could, through the Credit Award Transfer Scheme (CATS), transfer to universities on release. Many prisoner-students and offenders under supervision in the community who study other distance learning courses have the ability but not always 'real' opportunities to enrol at university. A university education is about more than accreditation it is an experience where many softer outcomes can be acquired. University education needs to be open to all; this will only occur when legislative change, clear guidelines and perhaps incentives are in place to prevent those with criminal convictions remaining forever on the periphery. Conversations with academic registrars illustrate ad hoc arrangements for making decisions on how applicants with criminal convictions are treated; this undermines the principle of a fair admissions procedure and does not aid rehabilitation.

As a society we are led to believe that education is one of the routes to successful, rewarding, and/or well remunerated, employment; if the Government commitment to reducing crime and the causes of crime is to be believed and widening participation to education, particularly higher education and university education, is to be a reality, not just a sound-bite, then we must ensure that those who have the ability can access the education that they merit. We must convey this message loud and clear, if those released from prison, whether at the end of a sentence, or on parole, are considered rehabilitated and/or punished, depending on your definition of prison and punishment, then surely they should face no added discrimination on applying for university courses. The limitations of the survey must be noted. The number of qualitative interviews was relatively small although the substantial amount of responses to the postal questionnaire supported the findings of the qualitative data and the methodology used.

Methodology

Mason (1994) advocates a mixed-method approach. This approach was chosen first as a response to the complexities when considering students with criminal convictions and the autonomous nature of universities. A second consideration was that the mixed-method approach enables methodological triangulation - propositions and theory can be developed out of the data under analysis (Denzin, 1989). The third and more practical reality arose due to budgetary and time limitations which prohibited the use of a large number of in-depth interviews. In keeping with the ideas of Glaser & Strauss (1967), it was felt that theory grounded in data would provide a useful starting point for future research or the formulation of policy and interventions at a later date.

Key stakeholders (including Higher Education Funding Council for England (HEFCE); Association of Chief Police Officers in England, Wales & Northern Ireland (ACPO); Criminal Records Bureau (CRB); Information Commissioner's Office (ICO); Association of Heads of University Administration (AHUA); Universities UK; Universities and Colleges Admissions Services (UCAS); Department for Education and Skills (DfES); National Union of Students (NUS); and the Chartered Institute for Personnel Development (CIPD)) were identified and then approached by letter. On the basis of the responses received a questionnaire was designed for those responsible for admissions procedures at the universities. A semi-structured interview schedule was devised for those who had applied to universities with criminal convictions. Both, telephone and face-to-face interviews were used in the research. There are many types of research triangulation, the between method approach seemed most expeditious in this research, combining dissimilar methods to illuminate the same class of phenomenon. In this case the questionnaire responses identified themes which helped structure the qualitative in-depth, semi-structured, interviews (Denzin, 1989; Mason, 1994).

Results

The results were derived largely from responses to letters, information gathered from paper questionnaires sent to universities, and verbal responses to semi-structured interviews with students in higher education. In particular students and the Coordinator of the Open Book project were most helpful in sharing their experiences of an innovative and unique scheme that engages individuals who may otherwise be excluded from fulfilling their potential.

"Any account of widening participation and lifelong learning should take account of the social as well as the economic benefits of education" (Thomas, 2000: p. 96). In this world we must hold onto the belief that education can do more than enhance career or work opportunities. Education has an intrinsic value; true education is less concerned with qualifications and accreditation and more concerned with self-identity and self-fulfilment. The results found that many universities were keen to have clearer guidance from informed professionals; those students who had experienced the Open Book project at Goldsmiths College were eager that others could benefit from such a scheme.

The questionnaires

A postal questionnaire was designed with both open and closed questions and sent to a random selection of universities. The sampling frame used was the UCAS universities list. Fifty-four institutions were contacted in the United Kingdom and questionnaires were sent to nine universities within Europe whom the Forum on Prisoner Education had contacts with through the European Prison Education Association (EPEA). Twenty institutions in the United Kingdom and two from Europe responded to the questionnaires.

Nineteen universities sent back copies of their written guidelines for dealing with applicants who have criminal convictions. Many of the documents received, and currently in use at the universities sampled, were written prior to 2005 and some were over six years old. There were considerable differences in the written policies returned. Two universities indicated in the space provided at the end of the questionnaire their commitment to engaging with and accommodating offenders as a means to reduce the likelihood of offending in the future. A further two universities are proactive in engaging, through widening participation initiatives, with offenders and prisoners or those who once bore those labels. They achieve this by making use of university funds or through applications and funding from external sources such as the European Social Fund (ESF).

There were five themes contained in the questionnaire:

1. Procedures for selecting applicants
2. The use of written guidelines
3. Access to criminal conviction information
4. Training of those who assess the applications
5. Assessing accuracy of application information

Theme one: whilst the overwhelming majority of universities had written guidelines in place for selecting applicants with criminal convictions, the content of these guidelines varied considerably. In some cases the written information provided in response to the questionnaire was dated and did not reflect the changes that have taken place especially with the re-design of the UCAS university application form. Whilst greater support could be offered to universities by those bodies having knowledge and experience of legislation concerning criminal convictions, or by working directly with those with criminal convictions, it is clear that having a written policy in itself does not necessarily ensure good practice. In one case, a university without a written code of practice was perhaps the most proactive and supportive university when engaging with those with criminal convictions.

Theme two: the majority of responses indicated that applicants were asked for additional information by letter although in a number of cases this was followed up when further information was elicited from face-to-face interviews. The individuals who had overall responsibility for making the decision on applicants with a criminal conviction varied across universities. In some cases there were two distinct processes in operation, one looking at the applicant from a purely academic view and the other assessing the relevance of the criminal conviction. In many cases the ultimate decision rested on the shoulders of one individual and in other cases a panel was convened that would assess on merit. In a small minority of cases the applicant would be initially assessed by an individual and then a panel would be convened at a later date if the applicant met the academic criteria.

Theme three: differing job titles made a direct comparison difficult, on some questionnaires more than one answer was given, in one case the procedure changed depending on whether the offence was considered 'minor' or 'major', although it was not clear who came to such conclusions. In many cases a group had access to the information and some cases it was an individual. In two cases the information was passed on only with the explicit consent of the applicant. In another case, unless a CRB check was required the information was destroyed at the end of the application cycle. A number of universities noted that provisions contained in the Human Rights Act 1998, the Data Protection Act 1998 and the ROA 1974 guided their policies. Whilst legislative recommendations are integral to the design of internal procedures, as a matter of good practice in some cases it was recommended that applicants who have criminal convictions could have a greater amount of consultation on the process on the process. It is also acknowledged that issues of safety and security must be weighed up against the potential for discrimination against applicants or successful candidates.

Theme four: indicated that there was an almost equal split between universities that provided no specific training for staff around assessing the suitability of applicants with criminal convictions and those that provided other training to staff that was designed to cover such issues. In two cases universities provided specific training for staff making decisions on applicants who indicated that they had criminal convictions. Given subjective attitudes to crime, offences and the stigma attached to (ex) prisoners and offenders, it would seem highly relevant that training should be provided for all those likely to be required to make decisions on the suitability of applicants.

Theme five: if the applicant indicates a conviction on the UCAS application form for 2006, section nine, there is still no guarantee that the information provided by the applicant to the university is correct. In the majority of cases universities would not check the accuracy of the information contained unless a conviction was indicated. In other cases the wording of the UCAS form indicating that it is the responsibility of the applicant to declare that the information is correct was considered a suitable check. In some instances applications that for some reason were considered doubtful were referred to the UCAS verification unit. In one case it was only seen as practical to check the validity of the information given when a CRB check was required as a routine requirement of the course. It seems that financial costs were too prohibitive to check all applications. There may well be cases where applicants who fail to mention criminal convictions are processed without such information being a consideration.

Good practice but not common practice

"The more closely and clearly we specify particular learner-subjects, the more likely we are to identify forms and processes of power that limit their options within everyday settings and to envisage or negotiate learning processes and outcomes in line with the ends that we seek" (Freire, 1994: p. 166).

As recent research points out, "the most disadvantaged young people tended to pay more for their education. With parents unable to subsidise them, they owed a higher proportion of their debt to banks and credit card companies, without facility to defer payments. The need to service these debts hindered their career planning and forced them to accept any job available" (Furlong & Cartmel, 2005: p. 1). The findings of the study showed that the political rhetoric purporting to encourage wider participation in higher education and greater access to universities is just that. Until better thought out funding arrangements coupled with more inclusive initiatives are worked out the fair access for all will remain a myth.

Open Book aims to make university education open to as many as possible. Joe Baden, the Coordinator, is changing lives and as a result generations through this programme. Semi-structured interviews were conducted with four students from the Open Book project, two with criminal convictions and one who had been in prison on remand. A telephone interview was conducted with another student who had attended university with a criminal conviction that will never be 'spent'. All of the names of those interviewed respondents have been changed to pseudonyms.

Massimo, now thirty-three, received a four week sentence in a local prison, and prior to imprisonment he had commenced a BTEC diploma. It was through the Probation Service that Massimo was referred to the Open Book project and with the support of Joe accommodation was secured and Massimo was accepted onto a course at Goldsmiths College, University of London. Currently he worries about continuation of funding to complete this course that has moved him away from crime and his criminal behaviour. In Massimo's words, "My self-confidence and self-awareness has increased. I needed a great deal of help to beat the pressure that was building up on me but I feel now that I have moved on. Teachers should have the skills of educational psychologists or counsellors; they should be more than teachers".

Julian, now twenty-five, was out of school at the age of fifteen and by sixteen he was in prison at a Young Offender Institute. He became involved in the Open Book project on a later sentence when referred by another organisation. Julian's prior learning was a BTEC national, the equivalent qualification to two A-levels. In Julian's words, "the Open Book project changes lives through the practical support and encouragement that it offers. It is a project that should exist in major cities in the country. This project needs to happen". Julian has real concerns over a lack of money that he has. Debt is a real problem and funding is an issue; he is waiting for a Local Education Authority grant. By taking one day at a time and working as a peer mentor at a pupil referral unit Julian has found that he can put something back and that young people identify with him. His criminal past is not a problem to this employer and it adds to his work. Julian candidly acknowledged that many of the real criminals that he has met have never had so much as a caution by the police.

Ashley was – in his own words – sent to a "special school" and had a wholly negative experience of education. He felt that once he had been picked out and labelled at school the whole process became a perpetual cycle. He felt his criminal past hindered his opportunities. Although never convicted and sentenced to a prison term, he has been remanded twice. Ashley has had significant problems accessing higher education mainly because of financial issues and housing problems. Ashley would like to see space created for people excluded from society. He believes that education should be tackled and a comprehensive assessment of needs must be followed up by individually tailored support. Education should be about breaking down barriers.

Ashley believes that the Open Book project is needed because the Probation Service does not offer this personalised service. For many in positions like Ashley's, the Open University does not offer the same level of support as it does not provide the student with an individual who understands the lived experiences. This is where the Open Book project makes a difference. The vast cost of prisons and the huge cost of community service and their failure to address re-offending behaviour make it all the more vital that the £3000 - £4000 needed to sustain the Open Book project is found. This project benefits generations afterwards by letting them into education. In Ashley's words, "all universities should have links with an outside project like Open Book. It should not be run by academics but by the people that know; those who have lived the life and understand the difficulties".

As the interview with Joe reveals, twenty-seven participants have come through the Open Book project to date and approximately 80% have criminal convictions. *Aim Higher*, a DfES initiative, provided limited funding to the project in the early days although further funding is now required as the project is so successful. Whilst there is a need for other universities to have a project like Open Book project, consultation with Goldsmiths College is required to ensure that the good practice is replicated. Individuals and universities need to understand the angle that Open Book is coming from. People must be aware of who Open Book is trying to get through the doors of higher education. Joe believes that the current UCAS application form encourages deception, "the matter of paramount importance is how the individual institutions process the information. Some universities are very positive in widening participation and including non traditional learners. There are equally some universities that are very poor at doing this. The benefit of the Open Book project is that it encourages honesty and offers support, guidance and in nearly all cases a place at university".

Educated by Europe?

Ragin (1994) believes the comparative approach can be summed up as having these important features: the use of flexible frameworks in which to work; a focus on diversity and the causes behind the diverseness; a systematic analysis of patterns by analysing both similarity and difference. A report by the Council of Europe Committee into Prison Education noted the importance of enabling those participating in prison education to continue with it on release. The importance of referral networks, availability and in particular educational advice and counselling was viewed as crucial to ensuring that those released prisoners - individuals with criminal convictions - have the support mechanisms in place to help them tap into education in the community (Council of Europe, 1990).

"A Norwegian submission to the Committee recognised that many who are students in prison fail to make the difficult transfer to ordinary education outside. In order to counteract this situation, follow-up/aftercare classes have been established at several different places in the country" (Council of Europe, 1990: p. 49).

The Swedish perspective on education, one based on the individual needs of a prisoner and geared towards post-release preparation, is a welcome one, "Education has always been emphasised as an important tool that makes, directly or indirectly, for the reintegration of offenders into society" (Svennson & Somander, 1998: p. 141). In principle offenders have the same rights as other citizens in the community, the Swedes embrace and foster what is known as 'the normalisation principle', that is to say offenders are in almost all respects no different from other citizens.

Similarly when looking at attitudes towards disclosure and periods of rehabilitation, the European countries that responded, *Breaking the Circle (annex D,)* to specific questions around their disclosure arrangements seemed more enlightened: In Belgium, offenders can apply for sentences over five years to become spent after ten years; In Canada, a mechanism is in place for those convicted of offences to apply for pardons after a specified period of time; In Denmark, a central criminal register records information which is normally deleted ten years after the sentence has been served; In Estonia, an offender's details remain on a register for up to fifteen years, after which they are spent; In Finland, there is a drive to require organisations seeking information to demonstrate the need. In Greece, records are deleted after eight years, providing no re-offending has taken place and pardons can be applied for; In Hungary the offences become spent after a maximum of ten years and employers cannot obtain details of the offences; In Japan, the period is ten years for the more severe sentences; In Portugal offences remain on record for between five and ten years; In Spain, as soon as the sentence is served the conviction is considered spent although some offenders will face additional checks (Home Office, 2002).

Conclusions

Whilst there is a growing body of research into desistance and assessments of 'what works', research into how a criminal conviction negatively impacts on the chances of an ex-offender or ex-prisoner to turn around their lives has been very limited, locally, nationally and internationally. Scant examples of good 'redemptive' practice are found in the Nordic countries; the beacons shining a light. The United Kingdom's punitive response in dealing with crime, criminals and criminal convictions undermines the pronounced commitment to provide a safer society for its citizens; when compared to European member states it is an embarrassment. Human Rights legislation protecting ex-offenders is the desired utopia, that legislation has not yet replaced the ROA 1974 gives huge cause for concern. By specifically including the prohibition of discrimination based on criminal conviction and ensuring any periods of disclosure are substantially reduced societies demonstrate a commitment and willingness to provide opportunities for individuals to genuinely move beyond their criminal pasts, and yet in England and Wales we do not.

Terms such as 'knowledge society', 'learning society' and 'learning journey', depict a life long pursuit of learning, rather than a career for life. In the post-modern society in which we live, an investment in human capital through education and training must be based on flexibility and individuality. Educational institutions are under a duty to safeguard the health and safety of all members of their communities, and should therefore think carefully before admitting a student who may pose a risk of harm to that community. It is clear that each case must be treated on merits, and all the circumstances have to be taken into account. What is also clear is many universities, in this risk-averse environment, are not mirroring the examples of good practice such as those operated at Goldsmiths College, Hull University and Leeds Metropolitan University, all of whom have provided opportunities for individuals with criminal convictions.

If we are really to change our society then we must do all that we can to move away from the principle of 'least eligibility' (Rutherford 1986). If we wish to reduce patterns of offending and re-offending, then those in prison and those leaving with criminal convictions should have access to more, not less, in order that as a humane society we lead by example. This argument is not solely principled, it is economic as well, "A former prisoner who re-offends costs the criminal justice system an average of £65,000 up to the point of re-imprisonment, and, after that, as much as £37,500 each year in prison" (DfES, 2005: p. 11). Weiss (1995) believes that it is only by providing individuals with access to conventional opportunities that we can hope for them to pursue legitimate occupations.

We must move expeditiously to re-focus offender education away solely from the 'Skills for Life' agenda. At present, we effectively bar an individual's progression in prison which could be a stepping stone into higher education in prison through distance learning, or in the community through a university education. Under the current arrangements, society discriminates against those prisoners on remand, those who have a higher prior level of attainment, women, black and minority ethnic groups. Poor financial support for those in education and a lack of joined up organised pastoral care in the community exacerbates the problems. Individuals who begin or continue education in prison are less likely to be able to benefit from opportunities in traditional universities. There is relatively little mention of higher education in a recent joint DfES document, *Reducing Re-offending Through Skills and Employment*. It is to be hoped that universities will be encouraged to support the growing number of ex-prisoners, ex-offenders, and offenders who have criminal convictions, into higher education, rather than assuming that they will desist from crime when they have gained a few 'Skills for Life' qualifications.

Freire (1996) reminds us that nobody lives outside our society. As Duguid (2000) iterates, the released prisoner is expected to undertake an active commitment to citizenship, and there must be a renewed commitment by society to assist those ex-prisoners in living by the rules attached to citizenship. Many citizens who have not been labelled prisoners or criminals display with regularity the very lack of values; compassion, humbleness, reverence, responsibility, co-operation and respect for community, they expect of the released prisoner attempting to 'go straight'.

The provision of a high quality prison education is not a frivolous use of resources. The former criminal wishing to transcend unconventionality has to aspire to a higher sense of responsibility for 'self' and community; to err once more means that the implications for individuals and the collective are dire. The former prisoner knows this more than anybody. If we are to ask those with criminal convictions to become full and active members of the community then we must provide the currency for them to achieve our ambitions and fulfil their responsibilities to themselves and society (Duguid, 2000).

The question for modern society is not, should we invest time and money to shape policies and foster practices that will ensure that a continuation of access to education at the highest levels is ensured for those who have been condemned as the most undeserving? But rather, how do we do this for it would be both politically expedient and morally responsible to do just that; society must offer true redemption for past actions for the benefit of future generations and opening up university education to all, legislative change, greater political encouragement, a more responsible media and more funding for qualitative research could achieve a situation that would turn the present barriers into mere obstacles.

In the hard sell arena the public are bombarded with the idea that the prison industrial complex in all its guises can provide a solution leading to crime reduction. This fallacy must be revealed for what it is. Community prisons (Home Office, 2005) were recommended in the nineties. The prison population at present does not allow for this. Other than solving social deprivation overnight one of the better ways to encourage incremental change is through education that opens up and captures hearts and minds. The exclusiveness that pervades society can be reduced by education and we must provide a clear pathway that helps, rather than hinders, the progress of the ex-prisoners wishing to make a career in education, training and information, advice and guidance, not laying pipes, their vocation. Now that the Learning & Skills Council is responsible for offender education, couldn't prisoners reasonably expect seamless provision when they are seamless managed under NOMS? If this cannot be assured what is the value of the 'going straight' compact they are expected to sign?

Bibliography

Council of Europe (1990); Education in Prison. Strasbourg: Council of Europe.

DFES (2004); Fair Admissions to Higher Education: Recommendations for Good Practice; Nottingham: Department for Education & Skills.

DFES (2005); Reducing Reoffending Through Skills and Employment. London: The Stationery Office.

Duguid, S. (1998); Final Report of the Prison Education Research Project. Canada: Simon Fraser University.

Duguid, S. (2000); Can Prisons Work? The Prisoner as Object and Subject in Modern Corrections. London: University of Toronto Press.

Farrall, S & Sparks, R (2006); Introduction; in Criminology & Criminal Justice; Vol 6, No 1; London, Sage Publications.

Fletcher, D., Taylor, A., Hughes, S., & Breeze, J. (2001), Recruiting and Employing Offenders. York: Joseph Rowntree Foundation.

Friere, P. (1994); Paulo Freire on Higher Education. In H. Giroux and P. McLaren (Eds.). New York: State University of New York Press.

Freire, P. (1996); Pedagogy of the Oppressed. London: Penguin.

Furlong, A., & Cartmel, F. (2005); Graduates from disadvantaged families: early labour market experiences. York, Joseph Rowntree Foundation.

Hamlyn, B., and Lewis, D. (2000); Women Prisoners: A Survey of their Work and Training Experiences in Custody and on Release. London: Home Office Research, Development and Statistics Directorate.

Harper, G., & Chitty, C. (2005); The Impact of Corrections on Reoffending: A Review of 'What Works' (Second edition). Home Office Research Study 291. London: Home Office.

Home Office (2002); Breaking the Circle – A Report of the Review of the Rehabilitation of Offenders Act. London: Home Office Communications Directorate.

Home Office (2003); Managing Offenders, Reducing Crime: A New Approach. London: Prime Minister's Strategy Unit.

Home Office (2005); A Five Year Strategy for Protecting the Public and Reducing Reoffending; London: The Stationery Office.

House of Commons (2005), Seventh Report from the Education and Skills Committee: Prison Education: Session 2004 – 2005. Volume I (HC114-11). London: The Stationery Office.

Hughes, E. (2004), Free to Learn? Prisoner-Students' Views on Distance Learning. Mitcham: Prisoners' Education Trust.

Ingleby, S. (2005), Time for a new diet?, Forum News, Issue 6, p. 5. London: Forum on Prisoner Education

Kanzawa, S., & Still, M. (2000); Why Men Commit Crimes (and Why They Desist), Sociological Theory, Volume 18, pp. 434-447.

Lam, H., and Harcourt, M. (2003); The Use of Criminal Record in Employment Decisions: The Rights of Ex-offenders, Employers and the Public, Journal of Business Ethics. Volume 47, pp. 237-252.

Morgan, M., and Kett, M. (2003); The Prison Adult Literacy Survey. Dublin: Irish Prison Service.

Nacro (2002); A simple guide to the Rehabilitation of Offenders Act 1974. London: Nacro.

Pawson, R. (2000); The Evaluator's Tale, in Wilson & Reuss (Eds.). Prisoner Education – Stories of Change and Transformation. Winchester: Waterside Press.

Prison Reform Trust (2005); Bromley Briefings - Prison Factfile May 2005. London: Prison Reform Trust.

Quinn, J., Thomas, L., Slack, K., Casey, L., Thexton, W., & Noble, J. (2005); From life crisis to lifelong learning: Rethinking working-class 'drop out' from higher education. York: Joseph Rowntree Foundation.

Ragin, C. (1994); Constructing Social Research. California: Pine Forge Press.

Rutherford, A. (1986); Prisons and the Process of Justice. Oxford: Oxford University Press.

Social Exclusion Unit (2002); Reducing Reoffending by Ex-Prisoners. London: Office of the Deputy Prime Minister.

Svensson, S., and Somander, L. (1998); Developments in prison education in Sweden, in W. Forster (Ed.). Education behind bars – international comparisons. Leicester: NIACE.

Taylor, S. (Ed.) (2005); Directory of Offender Education 2006. London: Forum on Prisoner Education.

Thomas, L. (2000); "Bums on Seats" or "Listening to Voices": evaluating widening participation initiatives using participatory action research, Studies in Continuing Education. Volume 22, Number 1. pp. 95–113.

United Nations (2002); Human Rights – A compilation of international instruments. New York: the United Nations.

Weiss, R. (1995); Prison Higher Education and the American Dream, in H. Davidson (Ed.). Schooling in a Total Institution. USA: Bergin & Garvey.

The 'Politics' of Prison(er) Education

Steve Taylor

The clearest indicator yet that prisoner education had become a political issue was in 2005 when it was mentioned twice in as many weeks on the BBC's current affairs programme, *Question Time*. In the second instance, Baroness Shirley Williams answered a member of the audience critical of 'mollycoddling' prisoners by talking of the importance of education as a means of rehabilitating prisoners and of demonstrating the way in which education can contribute to the fabric of a civilised society.

Any public or social policy issue becoming 'political' is not, of course, automatically a good thing. Witness, for example, the increased politicisation over recent years of child protection, hospital finance, or war. But the process of politicisation *can* have a positive impact, and in this chapter I will demonstrate that for prison education, an increased political interest and awareness has been largely positive; indeed, positive enough for there to be a real need for it to be sustained into the future.

Right place, right time

Although founded in 2000, the Forum on Prisoner Education had provided little more than a talking shop for a dozen or so individuals to meet and discuss the problems they perceived to exist in prisoner education. In 2003, however, these individuals – comprising academics, a prison education manager, and senior voluntary sector professionals – were encouraged by the Esmée Fairbairn Foundation, a large grant-making body, to register as a charity, appoint trustees, and apply for substantial funding to appoint a full-time Coordinator. Most founding members of the Forum became its first trustees.

When the present author arrived in post in January 2004, there remained some discussion among trustees of the newly-constituted charity about how to fill a full-time employee's diary; some had wondered if there was enough work to warrant a full-time worker. But just days after arriving in post, the then minister responsible for prisoner education, Ivan Lewis MP, announced that government was to abandon the five-yearly cycle of retendering for prison education contracts that was already six months overdue. This 'courageous' step would allow the Offenders' Learning & Skills Unit (OLSU) at the Department for Education & Skills (DFES) to consider how best to deliver and manage prisoner education in the future.

The minister's announcement that contracts were to be extended to allow OLSU to consider future options was the first significant movement in what was to become arguably the most turbulent two years in the history of prisoner education; it quickly became clear that the Forum on Prisoner Education was becoming established at just the right time.

Macropolitics – Parliament and Party Politics

The turmoil and uncertainty generated by the government's announcement that retendering had been abandoned but without any indication of what was to come provided increased focus for an ongoing inquiry into prisoner education by the All Party Parliamentary Group for Further Education & Lifelong Learning. Chaired by David Chaytor MP and with clerkship provided by the Association of Colleges (AOC), the Group had chosen prisoner education as the focus for its first detailed inquiry.

Taking evidence from various key players including the Chief Inspector of Prisons and the Director General of the Prison Service, and with a visit to Wandsworth prison in south London, the Group published an excellent report (APPG FELL, 2004) with wide ranging and well considered recommendations, many of which were supported by the Forum on Prisoner Education.

But such was the fast pace of the political interest at this time that, by the time the Group reported, the House of Commons Education & Skills Committee ('the Select Committee') had announced an inquiry into prisoner education – the first such inquiry since 1983 – and had begun taking evidence. Select Committees hold detailed inquiries and are a formal part of the parliamentary process; rather different to an All Party Group which are generally an informal grouping for parliamentarians interested in a particular subject: the focus of such groups range from children to whisky.

It was clear from the start that the Select Committee, chaired by the redoubtable Barry Sheerman MP since 2001, was to hold a detailed inquiry leaving no stone unturned. In the late spring of 2004, the Committee held an informal seminar for six professionals who could answer questions and allow members of the Committee to appropriately identify the real issues to be considered. These professionals included two Heads' of Learning and Skills, two ex-prisoners, and the present author.

Over the course of nine evidence sessions, the Committee heard from fifty-eight witnesses, and visited prisons in British Columbia, Finland and Norway, as well as five prisons and young offender institutions in England. In a significant departure from common practice, in order to facilitate the contribution of prisoners to the inquiry, the Committee took formal evidence from inside Feltham young offenders' institution. This is indicative of the thorough nature of the inquiry and the willingness of its members – all busy Members of Parliament – to commit to a full and detailed investigation.

Fifty-five recommendations were made in the Committee's Report (House of Commons, 2005a), which was published at the end of March 2005 together with a sizable volume of evidence (House of Commons, 2005b). (For a detailed précis of the inquiry and recommendations see Taylor (Ed.), (2005a).)

Not every Select Committee (of which there are more than two dozen) generates media attention. But along with the Health, Home Affairs, and Public Accounts Committees, the Education & Skills Committee regularly attracts media attention, not least for its willingness to criticise a government unequivocally committed to 'education, education, education'. In this inquiry, however, the Chairman was far from silent in his surprise and disappointment that on no occasion were members of the media to be found in the public area of the Committee Room, and he spoke of his frustration at the lack of media interest in an interview on BBC Radio 4's The Learning Curve programme (BBC Radio 4, 2005) almost two months after his report was published. Indeed, no newspaper covered publication of the Report and the only significant coverage was on news websites. Similarly, a report published by the Forum on Prisoner Education in March 2006, which included a review of the government's progress against the Committee's recommendations one year on, generated only limited media interest.

It is perhaps unfair, however, to berate the media for their apparent lack of interest. At the time of publication, at the very end of March 2005, speculation was rife about when the Prime Minister would call a general election, widely expected to be in early May. Hundreds of column inches were filled on a daily basis with the predictable pre-election conjecture and rumour; other 'political' stories took a back seat as a result. Six days after publication of the Report, the General Election was called, parliament was dissolved, and party politics sped on with exactly one month until polling day.

Whilst 'meta-issues' – such as big debates around health, education, housing and crime – dominate at election time, it was notable that 2005 was the first general election at which all three main parties (Conservative, Labour, and Liberal Democrat) extolled the virtues of prisoner education in their respective manifestos (Taylor, 2005b). This recognition of the importance of aspects of the penal system aimed at reducing reoffending was indicative of a wider shift in the politics of law and order (see, for example, Matthews & Young, 2003) that recognises, for the first time, that populist 'tough' policies are short-sighted and that to reduce crime, prisoners and those serving sentences in the community need to be given the skills and abilities that a significant number of them currently lack. No longer can we 'lock 'em up and throw away the key'; we need to do something to address the prisoner's needs – because the key is very, very rarely 'thrown away' and all but thirty-or-so prisoners will move back to live in the same communities as the rest of the electorate. This shift has been such that even those on the 'right', or who would not usually be expected to support measures that improve prisons, began to extol the virtues of prisoner education (Green et al, 2005).

The lack of media interest in the Select Committee Report was not, however, indicative of a wider lack of interest in the issue itself. Traffic on the website of the Forum on Prisoner Education increased by some 400% in the weeks before and after publication of the report. The volume of enquiries to the organisation also increased significantly, including a number from parliamentarians seeking further information, briefings and detailed statistics.

The publication of the Select Committee Report was welcomed by the Forum on Prisoner Education, but it was clear that publication of the Report had the potential to act as 'closure' to the issue; the point at which parliamentary interest ends. The obvious and visible passion with which members of both the Select Committee and, previously, the All Party Group had embraced the issue needed to be sustained in some way to ensure that prisoner education was not a 'flash in the pan' political issue, but rather, remained high on the agenda.

To this end, the Forum on Prisoner Education agreed to support Baroness Linklater, a Liberal Democrat member of the House of Lords, in establishing a new All Party Group to concentrate specifically on issues around prisoner education. The All Party Parliamentary Group for Offender Learning & Skills met for the first time in October 2005; in January 2006 the Group's name was changed to the All Party Parliamentary Group for Learning & Skills in the Criminal Justice System after concerns were expressed by some members of the Group that the original name excluded prisoners and those in the community who are innocent, or on remand. The change in name also allows the Group to consider wider issues with a direct impact, such as the training and development of prison officers.

The Group is open to members of both the House of Commons and House of Lords, has cross-party representation, and a number of independent members, including Lord David Ramsbotham, the former chief inspector of prisons, as one of four Vice-Chars. Members number over fifty, and observers attending meetings regularly count into the dozens. It may be indicative of the significance and importance of the Group that the minister responsible for this area of policy initially turned down an invitation to appear before the Group (although in his letter he acknowledged the importance of the new Group), but later asked for an opportunity to present a government Green Paper to the Group; this he did at a meeting in February 2006.

Most All Party Groups are supported by, and have clerkship provided by, a company or voluntary organisation relevant to the sector (the Prison Reform Trust, for example, provides clerkship to the All Party

Penal Affairs Group) and the Forum on Prisoner Education provides clerkship to this new Group.

Questions are frequently asked about exactly how significant All Party Groups are, and how much 'clout' they have. At the time of writing, this new Group has met five times and has already built a reputation as a significant contributor to the scrutiny of prisoner education – and beyond – and, it is hoped, this will continue into the future as changes to the delivery of 'offender learning and skills' take effect under the new Offenders' Learning & Skills Service (OLASS).

Micropolitics – Establishments, Quangos and Government

Recent changes in prisoner education have led to a number of 'political' debates and, some would say, disputes, taking place, from the level of the prison establishment up to departmental level within government. These different levels of micropolitics are not exclusive; all impact upon one another and are intrinsically linked.

Four years ago, the Youth Justice Board introduced a new post in juvenile young offender institutions (YOIs), that of Head of Learning & Skills (HOLS), whose role would be to act as an umbrella covering all learning and skills activity in the establishment, including the traditional education provision, libraries, workshops, and other regime areas with a learning and skills relevance. The success of the HOLS – who, crucially, is a member of the establishment's Senior Management Team (SMT) – in the juvenile estate led the OLSU to consider their implementation in the adult prison estate. With several million pounds of funding channelled into the Prison Service from the DFES, this began to take place in 2003; by early 2004 all establishments had a HOLS in post.

The recruitment of HOLS was, however, not without difficulty. Each prison recruited its own HOLS, and whilst individual governors were given a budget and a rough idea of the remit of the new post, there was a lack of clear direction over their role. As a result, many HOLS were appointed and found themselves responsible for something; but the 'something' was rather vague and a number were left to sink or swim. HOLS who were previously the Education Manager of an establishment generally fared better, having a clear idea of prison culture, but those recruited from outside (a significant number came from the mainstream further education sector and were new to prisons) were, in the words of one somewhat disenchanted HOLS who left her job, "left high and dry, trying to work out what our job was".

Prior to the appointment of HOLS, the most senior person in the establishment with direct responsibility for education was generally the Education Manager. Employed by the external provider holding the contract for education delivery in the prison, she or he would liaise with the governor and manage the delivery of education within the prison. A number of Education Managers applied for the new post of HOLS; others saw it as a betrayal of principles. In a number of cases, Education Managers became resentful of the HOLS who they saw as a barrier between them and the governor; someone interfering with the accepted norm of what had been delivered for years without any external scrutiny other than an inspection every two or three years.

In some cases, a deep resentment developed between the Education Manager and the HOLS. This, in turn, led to a number of Education Managers and HOLS quitting for an 'easier life' elsewhere. Indeed, one HOLS once told the present author that she was pleased she had "managed to drive that useless scumbag [the Education Manager] out" of the prison. A number of stories of bullying – of HOLS and by HOLS – were reported to the Forum on Prisoner Education. Thus a political resist-ance developed in a number of establishments which made life difficult for both the Education Manager and the HOLS.

Whilst recognising the importance of the HOLS, and their success in the majority of prisons, the Forum on Prisoner Education has called for providers to be funded appropriately in order to retain the post of Education Manager. In June 2005, accompanying a petition calling for the Education Manager's post to be safeguarded, a letter to the Prime Minister (Forum on Prisoner Education, 2005) stated that:

- the role of the Education Manager is vital to the effective delivery of prisoner education;
- education department should be managed by a person not employed by the prison;

- that the role of the Education Manager complements the role of the Head of Learning & Skills; and
- that the role of the Head of Learning & Skills (and any deputy posts created) is to oversee the delivery of contracts, and not to manage tutors and other education staff.

The Forum on Prisoner Education began the petition after hearing that, in the South-West of England (where the Learning & Skills Council was adopting a radical new system of delivery of offender learning under OLASS), the Education Manager post would be lost in favour of a new 'Learning & Skills Coordinator', employed by the Prison Service, and in all but name a Deputy Head of Learning & Skills. Ultimately this campaign failed, and Education Managers in the south-west disappeared with the implementation of OLASS in that region in August 2005, although a number of former Education Managers 'crossed the floor' to become Learning & Skills Coordinators. Nonetheless, the Forum on Prisoner Education continues to maintain that an 'outsider' (i.e. not a Prison Service employee) should be directly responsible for managing education within the prison. The Forum says that the fact that education staff are 'outsiders' is one of the reasons why prisoners enjoy spending time in education and feel they can rely upon and trust those staff members. In short, they're not jailers and so they earn the respect of the jailed.

The Forum on Prisoner Education appears, to an extent, to have been proved right. At one open prison, the HOLS and the Learning & Skills Coordinator became the subject of a number of allegations from prisoners, although the Governor of that prison was unwilling to investigate unless the Forum on Prisoner Education disclosed the names of the prisoners making the allegations, an action that would be in clear breach of the confidentiality that prisoners should rightly expect of the Forum. The incident of the 'useless scumbag' Education Manager also came from the south-west region. The most difficulty in implementing OLASS have come from the south-west, although it is acknowledged that this is in part due to the bizarre model of delivery adopted in that region – a model comprehensively rejected by each of the other eight regions in England.

The politics of prisoner education have been muddied by the complex relationship between HOLS and Education Managers, caused in no small part by the lack of clear direction from HM Prison Service on the purpose and remit of this new senior manager role. This is not the fault of HOLS or the OLSU, but rather of HM Prison Service for failing to provide clarity. In November 2005, days before a seminar for HOLS organised by the Forum on Prisoner Education at which he had declined to speak (both the OLSU and LSC attended and spoke), Michael Spurr, a senior board member at HM Prison Service issued a letter to HOLS promising further development of their role, clearly as a result of the discussions likely to take place at a forum in which HOLS were able to speak openly and freely under the Chatham House Rule, and in which they could be critical of their employer. Interestingly, this letter also tells HOLS that their posts are secure – an issue of some concern to HOLS – but this statement in itself made a number of HOLS feel that 'as soon as the Prison Service says your job is safe, you know your days are numbered'.

The handover of responsibility for the delivery of offender learning and skills, and the design and implementation of OLASS, to the Learning & Skills Council (LSC) is the result of months of planning by the LSC, OLSU and Prison Service. This handover is also not without political significance.

The biggest quango (quasi-autonomous non-governmental organisation) in the country, the LSC was created in April 2001 with the vision that, 'by 2010, young people and adults in England will have the knowledge and productive skills matching the best in the world'. Its budget in 2003-4 was some £8bn. However, offender learning and skills was, until August 2005, the only area of adult learning that laid beyond its remit.

Historically, prisoner education has been the responsibility of the Prison Service which, until 2001, had a Chief Education Officer's Branch responsible for the delivery of prisoner education across the public sector prison estate. In 2001, responsibility was transferred to the Department for Education & Skills, where the Prisoners' Learning & Skills Unit was set up; this became the Offenders' Learning & Skills Unit in 2003. The OLSU was unique within DFES as the only Unit within the Department that was directly responsible for delivery and so, when Ivan Lewis MP announced the abandoning of the 'old' contracting procedures (see above), it was clear that government was considering how best to deliver offender learning and skills in the future.

In the summer of 2004, ministers announced that responsibility for delivery would be moved to the LSC. This made practical sense, not least as the LSC was responsible for all mainstream post-16 learning in England. It was about 'mainstreaming' offender learning with adult education, and thus the Offenders' Learning & Skills Service (OLASS) was born, with the remit to organise the delivery of offender learning in line with a new specification published by the OLSU, titled the *Offenders' Learning Journey* (DFES, 2004) (a separate version exists in relation to juveniles, written in conjunction with the Youth Justice Board). The OLSU would continue to exist as the 'policy guardian' for offender learning and skills, albeit with a much reduced staff.

In December 2004, the LSC issued an invitation to tender for those agencies and organisations interested in submitting bids for delivery of the new Service in three 'development' regions: the North-East, North-West, and South-West. The two northern regions were to be offered on a broadly geographic model not dissimilar from the existing arrangements. In the South-West, however, the contract was being offered on a modular arrangement whereby the curriculum and specification in the *Offenders' Learning Journey* was split into five units. Negotiations with shortlisted providers took place in early 2005, and contracts began in August of the same year. The whole process had taken less than nine months, a timescale described as 'breakneck' and later acknowledged by the LSC's Jon Gamble, speaking to a meeting of the All Party Parliamentary Group in January 2006, to have been too short to allow for proper negotiations over issues such as staff contracts and pensions.

The contracting process for the remaining six regions in England – the 'developing' regions – began in late 2005 and was underway as this book went to press; delivery of the Service in these regions begins at the end of July 2006. The LSC was in danger of falling behind its own timescale again as they went silent over who had been successful in each region. The rumour mill was working at full speed.

Such silence was not surprising. Obvious difficulties in the transfer of responsibility have been exacerbated by a complete lack of communication from the OLSU and LSC with those at the front line of delivery. Complaints about this breakdown were a standard feature in discussions at the Forum on Prisoner Education's regional 'Talkshops', attended by several hundred tutors, Education Managers, and HOLS in 2005. All three parties involved in the new Service (OLSU, LSC and HM Prison Service) denied responsibility for keeping people informed. The OLSU said that it was the job of the LSC to tell people what was happening; the LSC insisted that it wasn't their job as the new Service was not yet operational; and the Prison Service said that the OLSU and LSC were better placed than they were to issue information and communications. A weekly email newsletter from the Forum on Prisoner Education has been credited by many staff as the most regular and effective source of information on the new Service.

The speed of the contracting process, a lack of consultation with those at the front line, combined with a wholesale failure in communicating with tutors, Education Managers, HOLS and providers have combined to leave many people in prisoner education feeling, yet again, that they are part of a 'Cinderella service'; that they are not as important as their colleagues working in mainstream adult education. In some areas, this has led to a haemorrhaging of highly qualified and experienced tutors who leave prison education for the relative security of a college or other educational institution. Concerns over lack of job security, a constant in prisoner education since the beginning of contracting in the early 1990s, have not been helped by new OLASS contracts being let for three years, rather than the five years under the outgoing system.

The involvement of four separate agencies – the LSC, OLSU, Prison Service, and the emergent National Offender Management Service - in prison education has not helped to stem the confusion. Three government departments have a responsibility – the Department for Education and Skills, the Home Office and, increasingly, the Department for Work and Pensions. As the Select Committee found (House of Commons, 2005a) there to be 'little sense of ownership of prison education, no obvious high profile champion within the DFES, and no drive or energy in moving things forward'. This is not surprising, when ownership could lie with four agencies or, at a higher level, with three government departments.

A further cause of confusion relates to what is *not* included in the new Service. Prisons and probation in Wales are excluded (the LSC does not cover Wales) and so responsibility has been transferred back to the Prison Service. Private prisons nationally are excluded, as is the children's secure estate. School-age children and foreign nationals are normally outside the LSC's remit, but they have been granted a dispensation for both groups where they are in custody. The debate over how higher education (also outside the LSC's remit) and some distance learning will be funded continues.

Just as those working in 'offender learning and skills', whether in prison or probation, were becoming familiar with the shape of OLASS, the government muddied the water even further by publishing a green paper, *Reducing Reoffending through Skills & Employment*, that threatens to abandon OLASS completely at the end of the first contracts in 2009.

Conclusion: Back to the Future

Prisoner education exists in an almost constant state of change. From 1992 to the present day, tutors, managers, governors and providers have had to endure numerous changes in the shape of the curriculum and the models of delivery. Whilst the development of OLASS could put in place a strong foundation for the future, it seems that government might not allow even this multi-million pound Service and accompanying infrastructure to bed down and show its worth.

The work of the Commons' Education & Skills Committee brought a great deal of attention to prisoner education; attention that is to be sustained by the ongoing work of the new All Party Group. That Group, together with organisations such as the Forum on Prisoner Education, Howard League for Penal Reform, and Prison Reform Trust, will ensure that prisoner education remains on the political agenda, and that government departments don't try to deny their responsibilities.

The need for consistency is critical and has never been greater. As the Social Exclusion Unit reported in 2002, prisoners who take part in education are three times less likely to reoffend after release. Increasing the education of prisoners is to increase the likelihood of their successful rehabilitation; it does not exist to increase the likelihood of a prison achieving its targets. Whatever model or arrangement is in vogue with government, the focus of 'prisoner education' must remain on the prisoner him or herself. Politicians, civil servants and others must ensure that before embarking on more change for the sake of change, it will lead to a real, tangible benefit for the prisoner student – the very person for whom prisoner education exists and who must be placed at the centre.

Bibliography

All Party Parliamentary Group for Further Education & Lifelong Learning (APPG FELL) (2004); Inside Track – Prisoner Education in 2004. London: APPG FELL.

BBC Radio 4 (2005); The Learning Curve. Broadcast 24/05/2005.

DFES (2004); The Offenders' Learning Journey. London: Department for Education & Skills.

Forum on Prisoner Education (2005); www.fpe.org.uk/filestore/emcletter.pdf

David Green, Emma Grove & Nadia Martin (2005); Crime & Civil Society. London: Civitas, the Institute for the Study of Civil Society.

House of Commons (2005a); Prison Education: Seventh Report of Session 2004-05, Volume I, HC114-I. London: The Stationery Office.

House of Commons (2005b); Prison Education: Seventh Report of Session 2004-05, Volume II, HC114-II. London: The Stationery Office.

Roger Matthews & Jock Young (Eds.) (2003); The New Politics of Crime and Punishment. Cullompton: Willan Publishing.

Taylor, S (Ed.) (2005a); Directory of Offender Education 2006. London: Forum on Prisoner Education.

Taylor, S (2005b); Prisoner Education: An Election Issue?; in Forum News; Spring 2005; London: Forum on Prisoner Education.

Index

Recommended Further Reading

The following titles may be of interest to those wishing to explore the subject of prisoner education in more detail.

Julia Braggins & Jenny Talbot (2003); Time to Learn: Prisoners' Views of Prisoner Education. London: The Prison Reform Trust.

Julia Braggins & Jenny Talbot (2005); Wings of Learning: Prison Officers and Prisoner Education. London: Centre for Crime & Justice Studies.

Howard Davidson (Ed.) (1995); Schooling in a Total Institution – Critical Perspectives on Prison Education. Oxford: Greenwood Press.

Stephen Duguid (2000); Can Prison Work? The Prisoner as Object and Subject in Modern Corrections. Toronto: University of Toronto Press.

William Forster (1995); Education Behind Bars: International Comparisons. Leicester: NIACE.

Howard League (2001); Missing the Grade: Education for School-Age Children in Prison. London: Howard League for Penal Reform.

Emma Hughes (2004); Free to Learn? Prisoner-Students' Views of Prisoner Education. Mitcham: Prisoners' Education Trust.

Steve Taylor et al (2005); Internet Inside. London: Forum on Prisoner Education.

Steve Taylor (Ed.) (2005); The Directory of Offender Education (2006 Edition). London: Forum on Prisoner Education.

David Wilson & Anne Reuss (Eds.) (2000); Prison(er) Education: Stories of Change & Transformation. Winchester: Waterside Press.

Further resources, including out of print policy documents and reports, can be accessed from the Resource Centre on the website of the Forum on Prisoner Education at www.fpe.org.uk.